RIPTIDES AND TAILWINDS

My Journey Through Sobriety, Forgiveness, Health, and Faith

For permission requests and ordering information, email the author at:
flboysells@aol.com

Book Design by: Jodi Costa
Cover Design by: Adrian Traurig

ISBN (book): 978-1-950995-07-3
Also available in Ebook

FIRST EDITION

Unless otherwise specified, Scripture quotations taken from
The Holy Bible, New International Version® NIV®
Copyright © 1973 1978 1984 2011 by Biblica, Inc. ™
Used by permission. All rights reserved worldwide.

Published by Two Penny Publishing
850 E Lime Street #266, Tarpon Springs, Florida 34688

ACKNOWLEDGMENTS

To my crew over at Two Penny Publishing:

Matt Gardner for making me sound better than I really am.

Adrian Traurig for an amazing cover and photos.

Holly Cole for correcting the mistakes I make.

Jodi Costa, the glue that keeps it all together, and the filter for when I get a little worldly. Meeting you through two great friends of mine (Greg and Jess Wilbur) was God sent.

Thank you to Tom Goodlet for teaching me the little things that mean so much in this process. I look forward to many more times to bond and build God's kingdom with you in the future.

To my Mom, Marlene, and Dad, Ed, for raising me somewhat right!

To my daughters for being so patient with me during my journey through darker times.

A special thanks to my buddy, Greg Wilbur, for being there for me during these times of riptides.

To the One and only One who creates the tailwinds.
To God, thank you for teaching me how to navigate
the rough seas of life. I look forward to every day
knowing you are my Captain.

TABLE OF CONTENTS

INTRODUCTION

This is a book I didn't want to write, but it's a book I had to write. In life, sometimes you experience things for others and sometimes you go through things for yourself. I would have to say this book is a little bit of both. Here is what I have learned along the way is:

1) God is really with you and I throughout the whole process of life. However, sometimes it will seem as though He is nowhere to be found.

2) I can honestly say from my experience that God has a plan for you and I, and during His plan, He will allow hard things.

Something you wouldn't want anyone else to have to go through. But it's during those times He is developing and refining your character. He's getting you ready for something great, something amazing. If He were to show you what it is it would be overwhelming and seemly unbelievable. However, when God's timing which seems to always be late by your own selfish ways and by worldly ways. When He delivers what it is that you have wanted for a long time, it is always on time and never just the way you thought it would be. It is always better and always overwhelming to the point of tears flowing down your face. And then you realize it could have never happened if you knew the truth the whole time. Chances are, you would have messed it up if you knew the truth. That is the beauty for the ashes.

I invite you to come along and see just what our amazing God has done for me. Once you see what He has developed in me, He too will start to do something in you that will simply overwhelm you. He is God and what He starts He always finishes. Trust me or better yet trust Him. Whether your life is in a "riptide" or a "tailwind", I can promise you there are smooth waters coming and the water is clear as it can be and all of the unknown will be known, according to His plan. Your hope will find faith and your faith will become something I can't explain because I can't explain what He is going to do in your life. Only He can!

CHAPTER ONE
WELCOME TO MY LIFE

September 2016

Not sure where to begin this whole crazy story… so let's start from the beginning. I have been drinking alcohol for more than 30 years of my life. I started back when I was 18 years old and have continued drinking through the years up until this point. Although, I've been drinking a little more heavily this time than I did back then. But that is how most things go in life, you either get better or worse over time and there isn't much that stays the same. To help paint a picture, let me tell you where I have been recently in regard to how much alcohol I drank. So, on an average day I'd drink a 12 pack of hard seltzer water called White Claw. We can call it beer, it has a similar percentage of alcohol by volume. Whenever I read the ingredients on the can, the "pure" and low-calorie contents, I would justify in my mind that it was actually healthy for me. Which I know is crazy but I'm kind of an alcoholic so there you go. Oh, and every now and then I would add shots of vodka at night to help me sleep (the more I needed to sleep the more shots I would take).

Was I an alcoholic? Absolutely; no question about that! Did I want to stop? Not really. I thought that everyone has problems, and so do I. Every family has problems, and so does mine. I convinced myself that I wasn't all that different than other people and that I was handling myself pretty well. All and all, things were pretty much "okay".

Then in September of 2016, it hit me like a hurricane. My wife was away on a business trip. That is hard enough, just to be away from her. Yes, because I do love her very much but also because our relationship was becoming more and more rocky. She was starting to let me know that my drinking was hurting her and our family. She once said, "I only get 25 percent of you and the other 75 percent you are drunk or drinking." And she was right. Not sure why I was blessed with such a great woman, I couldn't let alcohol screw up our marriage. When she did travel out of town on trips like this, she would go dark on me, meaning she wouldn't answer my calls or respond to my texts. I felt alone, left to take care of my business (I've owned a Tree and Landscape Co since 1998) and our home and kids as well.

So, I decided to take a day off of drinking… which did not go very well. Maybe I thought that the extra responsibilities demanded extra focus and I thought I could stomach an entire day of no drinking. I was wrong. I usually drink to numb the pain, but at this point my decision to not drink was causing me incredible pain and discomfort. I actually made it through the day without drinking; it wasn't comfortable, but I made it. But the next day was hell. I felt like I was having a heart attack! I actually had my parents take me to the emergency room at a local hospital. They kept me there and gave me a stress test. It wasn't a heart attack, but it sure felt like one. So, after a night in the hospital they let me go. They told me to get a hobby and focus on less stressful things. I am surprised that no one stated what was later obvious; this was the result of a sudden withdrawal from alcohol.

Detoxing is no joke. In the period of time when you first remove a substance from your system, your body will cry out for what it is used to getting. In reality, withdrawals can create a number of painful symptoms – some of which are extremely dangerous. In extreme cases, it is best to seek detox and experience withdrawals in a safe and professional environment where you can be monitored and taken care of. In my experience, I'm glad that I went to the hospital that night. However, at this point in my story I wasn't certain that I wanted to go through the detox experience. My first run in with withdrawal felt like hell, and I wasn't too eager to jump right back in.

So here I am, finishing up 2016 with my first real run-in with sobriety and it sucked. I'm an alcoholic. I drink to numb the pain I feel in my stomach when I wake up, I drink to get through the day, I drink to relax at home, and I drink to fall asleep at night. Even though I treat alcohol like a solution, I know that it has only brought me more problems and pains. I was out drinking one night when I was 22 years old when I was stabbed in the chest; proof that nothing good happens after dark. It was 3am in the morning and the man who stabbed me was on LSD. The knife missed my heart by ¼ of an inch and my lung by ¼ of an inch. The doctor said "if the knife hadn't been as sharp as it was, I most likely would have died." Thank

God for bad guys with sharp knives, right? I believe that there were many times when I should have died or been thrown in jail.

I had a toxic relationship with a toxic substance. Almost everything in my life revolved around drinking. Alcohol has touched all of my relationships. My marriage is heading in the wrong direction, again. I was married once before and was divorced almost 15 years ago. I pray that will be my only divorce. Divorce is like a hellacious withdrawal because you have to experience the sudden removal of something that was in your life and now is not. Some people are thankful for divorce, depending on their needs and circumstances, but in my experience, it's just awful.

While I was going through my divorce in 2002, I took a trip with a good friend who knew I was going through a hard time. We went camping up in Lake Tahoe, at a place called Emerald Bay. It is a beautiful state park in California and this was an incredible opportunity to clear my head and enjoy the beauty of God's creation. We went wakeboarding all day and then went back to the camp to hang out around the campfire. The next day, we went mountain climbing and then went and watched the fireworks from the boat in Lake Tahoe. It was, and still is, the best fireworks show I have ever seen. The fireworks were so close to us! Normally you feel like fireworks are a grand shared experience, but that night they seemed to just be for us. It was truly awesome. To end the exciting night, we decided to head up to the casinos. We had just been in Heaven watching those fireworks and then we were off to the devil's playground, or so they say.

After we were all done at the casino, we were ready to call it a night and head back to the campsite. It was past midnight and our best way back was by boat. Now I'll have you know summer nights in Lake Tahoe can drop to the low forties. The water at night can hover around 50 degrees. Alcohol was involved in the party that night, so I'm not sure how my friend (Colin) made his way out of the marina, but he did! So, we were off in open water on our way back to camp.

Suddenly, the boat stopped running. I remember seeing the thermometer, a chilling 39 degrees. It was close to 1am and we were now stuck in a small ski boat on Lake Tahoe at night. We tried all the tricks we knew to get the thing up and moving again with no luck. After thirty minutes we knew it was either a major engine issue that we were unable to fix or it we had somehow ran out of gas. It was just me, my friend, and his girlfriend (at least they could try to keep each other warm). I grabbed an oar and spent the next five hours trying to move our boat closer to shore.

The night grew impossibly dark and frigidly cold as I attempted to row the boat in any direction other than the middle of Lake Tahoe. A beautiful night, quickly demolished into a freezing nightmare! How can anyone help themselves in darkness? How can anyone steer their ship to shore when it feels like you are constantly getting pulled back out into depths of the water? My hands were numb, but I was too cold to stop, I needed the movement to stay warm. Welcome to my life, stuck in a dark place with little clue of how to get out, so I'll just do what I can do to get by until hope comes in the morning.

Have you ever felt that way? Have you ever felt stuck or caught in a loop of going through the motions over and over again with little to no hope for anything to actually change? I was in that loop of drinking to feel better, feeling bad, and drinking to feel better again.

I believe that at least three things have to happen in order for us to start heading back to shore. First, we have to want it. I spent five hours rowing on that lake. I was determined to do something in order to help improve our situation. The second thing we need is help. When the sun finally came up we spotted another boat off in the distance. Thank God it was a quiet morning so they could hear us yelling. They came over and towed us to the nearest marina. The third thing we need is to understand the problem. Once we got back to the marina we put gas into the tank and the engine started up. There was a chance that the gas was siphoned out of our boat, but we obviously didn't think to check it before we left the marina that night. We were upset to say the least.

You know, things in life go a whole lot smoother when you can grab a hold of those three things.

Determination to move in the right direction

Help along the way

A clear understanding of what is going wrong

If morning never came, I would probably still be out on Lake Tahoe rowing in circles. If help was available but we didn't seek it out, then we would have struggled to get anywhere productive. And if we got back to shore and didn't correctly understand the problem then we could have set off again only to get stuck a second, third and fourth time.

In September of 2016, I had my first taste of fighting with the riptide of alcoholism and it felt about as uncomfortable as being stuck on a lake in the middle of a cold night. My drinking won't calm down in the coming months, I'll return to my 12-18 drinks a day with some extra shots of vodka. But a point is coming soon when I know that a change needs to be made and I want my life to be different. I want to have the determination, the help and the understanding of how to fight the tide and navigate my life to a better place.

CHAPTER TWO

DETOX

March 26th, 2017

Today is Sunday and I just checked my blood pressure. I don't know what I expected, but I was not happy with the result. I clocked in at 135 (systolic) over 99 (diastolic), which is generally considered to be stage one of hypertension. They say that my level is near the point where my risk of heart attack, stroke, heart failure, or chronic kidney disease can double. I've said it before, things typically get worse or they get better. I can't afford to keep letting this get worse. I need to get better. I've been planning on it for a little while now, but the time is here and I feel more motivated than ever to try. So, I made the decision to stop drinking because I can see that it's not good for my health or my situation. I'm understanding more than ever that this is a major cause of what is wrong in my life. Alcoholism steals, kills, and destroys parts of your life. I convinced myself that it was helping but now I know better. The Bible says that the Devil comes to lie, steal and destroy – I believe that alcohol takes pages from the same playbook. It can seem harmless, normal and fun; you can tell yourself that you can't have fun without it. Everyone else is doing it, so why not you?

For many years, that is what I believed. Those thoughts are evidence that the Devil is getting a hold of you, and if you don't watch it he will get a hold of everything that matters in your life. Why? Because he only comes here to lie, cheat, steal, and destroy! If you can't eliminate his voice out of your mind, you will continue to believe that your brokenness is normal and justified. You will soon find yourself doing things you would have never in a million years thought you would do. Alcohol is one of the devil's most valuable tools because it slowly grabs a hold of you and pulls you out to sea. You need to replace that lying voice with a better one. You need a strong and steady tailwind. A peace that passes all understanding and judgment. As I seek to replace bad habits with good habits, I need to replace the Devil's lies with God's grace and truth.

March 27th, 2017

Now I would call this Monday the first day on my detox. Here is what I did! During the day I cut back on my consumption of alcohol to about half: probably 6-9 White Claws and zero Vodka. So, throughout the day I drank a lot less alcohol but, unfortunately, I did not drink a whole lot of water. I had heard that you can't quit cold turkey, so I thought it was best to wean myself off slowly by cutting my drinking in half. Even though I drank half of what I normally drink, the withdrawals started hitting me hard. By the time Monday night was turning into Tuesday morning, I was in intense pain. I got out of bed and threw up. My stomach was in so much pain and my heart wanted to leave my body.

March 28th, 2017

It is 1:30am and I am back in the hell of withdrawals. There is intense pain raging across my body. I'm freezing, like a fish in a cooler full of ice. I feel like I'm sinking deeper and deeper in icy water, the crushing weight and pressure of being dragged to the bottom of the ocean. My wife got up and we had a fight about how I should go about all of this. I had already contacted 3 or 4 rehab places but most were full. A friend of mine directed me to the best facility in the area, but beds don't simply open at will so I had to keep calling and hope for an opening. I called 5 times with no luck. I had managed to get a few hours of sleep throughout the night, but now I was back in bed fighting the cold sweats and intense pain in my stomach.

I laid in bed praying to God asking Him for help. I felt like He reminded me of something, a strange and random thing that I heard a long time ago. About 15 years ago, I attended a seminar in Mexico about holistic healing. I don't remember much about that seminar but there was one story that suddenly popped back into my head. There was a man speaking at this seminar and he shared this story. A three-year-old boy was struggling with stomach problems and had a lot of blood in his stool. The problem persisted, and they were becoming very concerned. He instructed them to give the baby cabbage juice. After two days of drinking cabbage juice the little boy no longer had any blood in his stool and was making a full recovery.

So, this story hits me as I'm laying in bed. I get up and find that I actually have a head of cabbage in my refrigerator. What are the chances of that? I cut up a piece of the cabbage, add some spring water and blend it in my Nutribullet. I drank the whole glass, and it tasted terrible! It's now just after 2:00am and my stomach and chest pains are starting to go away. It wasn't a full and immediate fix; I'm not saying that I was instantly healed. However, my stomach pain did start to subside, and I was able to get back into bed and fall asleep for a few hours.

I got up at 5:30am and went downstairs to blend up another glass of cabbage juice. Yes, it was gross but I was now determined. The past 24 hours have hurt like hell and I don't want it to be for nothing. I decided to weigh myself before I went to work, 189.8 pounds. My thoughts were focused: I'm going to detox all of this shit out of me today. Crazy, right? I'm still calling the detox center trying to get in. No luck yet.

I brought six bottles of water to work. My crew and I had a tree removal that day. I put on a long sleeve shirt hoping to sweat as much as possible. It took three and a half hours to take out the tree. During that time I drank all six bottles of water and I was actually feeling pretty great! Sure, I stopped 4-5 times and wasn't on my "A game" but I made it through the morning. I was working on an empty stomach, only cabbage juice for fuel (and a Snickers). Lunch came around. This is the time when I would normally want a beer or White Claw instead of eating a normal healthy meal. But today, I ate a whole sandwich and had Diet Dr. Pepper. I had no desire for alcohol. I believe that was due to the pain from the night before. I'm still feeling inspired to let that part of my life go. My journey has been 30 years long and this was the first time that I felt like the wind was at my back. I could do this.

After work I went straight home, no need for distractions. I worked hard today and I wanted to weigh myself again. To recap, I've had two glasses of cabbage juice, lots of bottles water, a sandwich, and a diet Dr. Pepper. After all of that, I weighed 184.8 pounds. I work landscaping in Florida, so I am prone to sweat some weight off during a hard day of work, but this was different. I lost five pounds since the start of the day. I don't know what all my body detoxed throughout the day, but it obviously let go of a lot of stuff that it didn't need or want.

As the day ended, I enjoyed dinner and felt great. No stomach pains, no heart aches. I had one more glass of cabbage juice and then slept for eight hours. Was it a miracle or just simple chemistry? I'm leaning towards both. I'm replacing alcohol with cabbage juice; I think it is better for me. I used to wake up in the morning and drink alcohol to numb the pain in my stomach. I know now that the alcohol was likely causing that pain in my stomach, likely a stomach ulcer. Well, cabbage juice is considered to be a natural remedy for ulcers. The cabbage juice has lots of potential benefits, I've definitely felt it. There is some science behind it but it is also a miracle that I remembered this remedy at this time in my life. I feel inspired to live a better and more sober life, and that inspiration is strong enough to get me to keep drinking this awful tasting vegetable.

Detoxing is all about removing the toxic elements from our body and making room for healthier things. There are lots of things to detox from, mine was obviously alcohol. What is yours?

I want to tell you about an incredible story that I was able to witness firsthand. It all goes back to a small town in California that was battling an invasive species of pike fish in their local lake. The heartbeat of this town centered on their pristine waters and scenery, fishing for trout and the tourism that came from it. The pesky pike were a danger to their trout and endangered salmon in neighboring bodies of water. It was a real problem that needed a solution.

Well, in 1997, the California Department of Fish and Game thought that the best course of action would be to poison the lake in order to kill all of the pike. Despite opposition from the town's residents, they moved forward with the plan and dumped 64,000 pounds of powdered rotenone and 16,000 gallons of fish-killing chemicals into the lake. The pike were successfully eradicated… along with all other aquatic life in the lake.

Other side effects arose, including traces of the poison finding its way into the town's water supply. The town fought back as best as they could, taking the department to court by filing claims against the state of California. There were varying stories of how well residents and businesses were compensated, or if they were compensated at all. I couldn't imagine how outraged I would be if this happened in my town. It actually gets a little worse, and this is where I enter the story.

Nineteen months after the lake was poisoned to eradicate the pesky pike, two pike were caught in the lake in one day. Talk about adding insult to injury. The residents were once again looking for a solution and I had an opportunity to help. I came up with a plan for the town to host fishing tournaments and spear fishing tournaments to get rid of their pike problem. I shared some recipes with them so they might be interested in doing some cooking competitions as well. I figure this could be a great idea, clear out the problem and replace it with something fun. As I stood in front of the crowd at the town hall a man spoke up. He said, "yeah well that might work, but if it does what will happen to our checks?" I was confused. One of the board members who was leading the town hall meeting explained to me that some people were receiving $15,000 a year in compensation. Some people were nervous that any attempts to fix the lake, which impacts everyone in town and neighboring towns, might result in a handful of people losing their checks. I knew that this community needed help, what I didn't know is they didn't all want help.

Nothing was fixed or resolved for years. Shockingly, the lake was once again treated with chemicals to kill the pike in 2007, ten years after the first round. There was some intent to take action, but in the end it was easier to let things be and allow more poison into their lives. Sounds familiar, doesn't it? I let alcohol invade my life for 30 years without a fight. I invited the poison in and it impacted more areas of my life than I would have hoped. This happens to so many of us. We allow a problem to exist and we don't know what to do, so we turn to a dangerous vice to fix it or fill it. We willingly choose poison over putting in the work that it takes to detox our body from it. If you are lonely, scared, anxious, angry or broken – don't choose poison over healing. Don't choose the status quo over making a change. Detoxing is hard and painful but continuing to put poison into your body will eventually kill you.

CHAPTER THREE
FORWARD PROGRESS

March 29th, 2017

Life is a journey and for the first time in a long time, I feel like I'm moving forward. I'm writing this book as I go, and at this point I don't quite know where I'm going yet. There is a famous Bible passage that comes to mind:

> *No, dear brothers and sisters, I have not achieved it,*
> *but I focus on this one thing:*
> *Forgetting the past and looking forward to what lies ahead,*
> *I press on to reach the end of the race and receive*
> *the heavenly prize for which God, through Christ Jesus, is calling us.*
> *Philippians 3:13-14 (NLT)*

I may not know where I'm going but I know that I don't want to go back to where I've been. I also know what is calling me forward: my faith, my family and my health. I've not yet figured everything out, but at least I have some direction: forward.

Part of letting go of the past means grabbing a hold of something new. I've mentioned my new relationship with cabbage juice, that is a new element in my life that is helping me move forward. Another new element is writing. I am writing these notes and entries as part of my day in hopes of eventually turning this into a book. I'm writing this morning on March 29th with some excitement for how I'm feeling both mentally and physically. It feels like I've experienced a miracle. It's now 5:31am; I don't think that I'm going to keep calling the rehab center today. Today I get to truly enjoy my morning and hopefully the rest of my day. My wife is getting out of bed and I get to make her coffee, and breakfast for myself as well.

I can't help but notice how much my attitude is changing. I'd normally wake up and feel sick and tired, then I'd have to get out of bed and I'd have to figure out my day. But now I get to, and that is a dramatically different state of mind. Do you feel the difference in your life, between the things you have to do and the things that you get to do? Some things just aren't as much fun as others, but just about any "have to" can become a "get to" with a healthy mindset. I get to help my kids get ready for school. I get to go to work. I get to drink another dank cup of cabbage juice. There are probably things in your life that used to be healthier, things that you used to feel excited or privileged to be part of. I'm a believer that it is all connected and if I can improve my physical health then my mental and emotional health can follow along with my body's progress.

April 3rd, 2017

This past weekend I had my first real experience with "peer pressure"
or temptation. My wife and I attend a fundraising event each year for one
of our daughter's schools. They have free food, drinks, live entertainment,
silent auctions and gambling tables. In the past, my wife and I would just
get pretty buzzed and have a good time; but this time, not a drop of alcohol
for me and out of respect, my wife only had one glass of wine.. I told her
I didn't care if she drank, it really doesn't bother me. While enjoying the
event, I noticed how some of the drunk parents acted and I could smell the
alcohol from everyone's breath. It was kind of disgusting. I couldn't help but
think, that is what I used to smell like all the time. It's kind of funny and
kind of sad because they probably don't realize how bad their breath is right
now.

This was an eye opening experience for me, and I feel like I'm
going to have many more of those as I move forward. So, it has been one
week since my detox and I feel great. I haven't thrown up, my stomach is
perfect and my heart feels just fine. I totally detoxed in two days! Over
the weekend, I had some great moments with my family; they were little
moments, but still very encouraging nonetheless.

April 5th, 2017

I had my blood pressure checked again. Ten days ago it was 135/99,
which is not very good. Today I came in at 111/78, which is great! I am still
feeling so much better, I haven't felt this good in years. I'm sleeping well

and enjoying life again. I have more confirmation that I was headed in the right direction. No strong desires to head backwards to my old lifestyle. Pretty happy with where this ship is headed. Still don't know where I'll end up but the water is better ahead of me than it is behind me.

One of the biggest lies that I had believed was that I couldn't have fun without drinking. To be honest, I was a child the last time that I believed otherwise. Today I once again believe that we can have just as much fun without alcohol (and we can actually remember our fun experiences afterwards). I went spearfishing for the second time this week. It is something that I love but hadn't done in over a year. I got three fish for dinner and came home to clean up and then went back out to play poker. Tomorrow, weather permitting, I will go kick footballs at the field down the street and run sprints back and forth retrieving the balls. Do you see what I'm doing? I'm replacing time that used to be dedicated to sitting around drinking with things that are more fun and better for me. Alcohol used to be a gateway for enjoyment and fun, but it was really holding me back from fully experiencing anything. I also believe alcohol is the true gateway drug. It numbs your senses and makes you do things you would never do sober.

My life was so screwed up that my mind had linked alcohol with sex. I'd start drinking and then my mind would assume that sex would be coming soon. I know that is a crazy and unrealistic thought now that my head is clear, but that is where my mind would often go in the past. The association of going out for drinks and having sex fueled my desire to drink. I'm hoping to stay in a more sober and mature mindset because I'm more aware now of how I used to think while under the influence.

April 9th, 2017

I haven't thrown up in 12 days. That is a good feeling. I just finished my cabbage juice. The recipe is evolving and now contains red cabbage, blueberries, half an apple, and random things that I want to clear out of the refrigerator (anything that will overpower the terrible taste of that cabbage). The juice has improved and so have I. What would you add to cabbage juice to make it taste better?

For lunch, I'm having turkey sandwiches on rye with mustard, no mayo. Sometimes I have a tuna sandwich with avocado. Dinner is usually chicken or seafood with salad and some kind of vegetable. Usually water is my drink of choice but every now and then I'll have an Arnold Palmer. My real weakness is that damn ice cream, it always calls my name late at night.

I'm taking supplements like Men's One A Day Vitamins, Vitamin B-12, and Milk Thistle in the morning, and at night I'm taking 10mg of Melatonin Gummies to aid my sleep.

I share all of this in hopes of giving you some ideas to aid your journey. What you put into your body, good or bad, will impact you. I feel good, and you can too! I've heard it said that it takes 22 days to start a new habit or pattern. I believe that this process starts by making choices, one day at a time, that ultimately transition into regular parts of your life. You can choose to stop doing something like drinking and/or start doing something like eating better. It's important to remember that the choice is up to you.

I used to look forward to the weekends because it was an open invitation to party and drink more than I normally did. Now all my weekends are consumed with my family and activities. Tennis lessons, golf, yoga class, and spearfishing, if I'm lucky enough to get away and shoot some fish. We are attending church every Sunday. Today, it's a pancake breakfast with the Easter Bunny. I don't normally eat pancakes but I'm bringing my own chocolate chips to add in, so now I'm eating pancakes. Just a little adjustment and the situation is much improved.

April 14th, 2017

Good Friday

Today I got up at 4:30 am because my daughters were up early. It's "Good Friday" and, for the first time in my life, it feels like a great Friday. I'm really looking forward to the day and the weekend. My whole family is coming over for Easter Dinner on Sunday. It should be a great time, a time of new beginnings. I'm so glad God pulled me out of where I was. I believe He can do it for anyone when they truly want to make a change.

I've been thinking about the idea that real changes take 22 days to really sink in. I don't know if it is true but I'm moving closer and closer to it. I do know that I was stuck but now I'm freer than I've been in a long time. I feel like my sailboat is being directed by winds I have never felt before. It is like I'm going to a place I should have been a long time ago. A place where all the bad stuff from the past will all make sense. This place is a place of peace and fulfillment. This place feels like home.

When was the last time you prayed? I mean really talked to God like he is your friend, because He is! He is that and so much more! How have you been taking care of yourself, your body and your mental health?

What about your car or truck? Is it clean and taken care of? Is your home being kept clean and properly maintained? In most cases, we do not have all of these things in order. No one is perfect! Think about this, why would God bless you with better health or peace of mind or financial stability if you're not taking care of what you already have? We have to assume some responsibility for where things are at, and when we ask God for help, we shouldn't expect Him to magically make everything better while we sit back and do nothing. In life, it's the little things that add up and can change your life for the better.

You don't have to fix everything overnight and you shouldn't ever count on making your life perfect. You can reach for the goal line and still get tackled hard. I like football, and forward progress is an important concept in the game. Forward progress is all about moving in the right direction. Forward progress is the concept of measuring how far you advance forward, despite being tackled and pushed backwards. So, you can know that a defender is coming to tackle you, but you will earn every yard you get, even if you get knocked down on your butt. If I run ten yards and get tackled backwards two yards, my forward progress is still ten. It is worth pushing forward because the only person that can take yards away from you is you! That is why coaches hate players that run backwards or sideways. Don't be afraid of failure or getting hit. Move forward and know that every inch of progress counts. And when you get hit, get back up and run again.

CHAPTER FOUR

MY RECIPE FOR A SUCCESSFUL LIFE

1. **GOD** MUST BE FIRST IN YOUR LIFE

Without Him we don't even exist. Question to ponder! What do you think about God? In my case, the follow up question is what do you think about Jesus? Your place in this universe definitely depends on these questions. If you don't have an answer, then I challenge you to consider this and take some time to seriously seek out some pastoral counsel from someone you trust.

I believe that God is real and alive. That He allows us to make big mistakes and face consequences, because He wants to help us tell a better story with our life. Jesus is the Son of God, our Savior, and He died for us so that we can have the ability to be renewed and transformed. We don't have to be stuck sinking in the depths of our sin, we can find peace and healing in Him. My recipe for a successful life begins here because if I can have a relationship with the God that created everything then I can find the strength and courage to do what I need to do in life. I know that God can help you tell a better story with your life.

2. CREATE **HEALTHY** HABITS

You really can't do much when you are unhealthy. You are a liability to yourself. You are stuck on a boat with one oar, paddling just to stay warm. On the opposite end, when you are healthy you can operate at your highest and best level. That way we can take care of others like our family and friends. We ought to eat right, avoid unhealthy things, exercise, and get proper sleep. It doesn't matter where you start, move in a healthier direction. Anything can be turned around. As I write this, I have lost 10lbs. I'm slowly working to get to my high school graduation weight; the key word here is slowly!

We don't become healthy overnight, and I didn't become unhealthy overnight either. It happens over the course of time as our daily habits carry us in one direction or the other. I've said it before and I'll say it again: you either get better or worse over time and there isn't much that stays the same. Habits are the key because they are the steady course setter for where you are going. You don't need to conquer your health as much as you need to conquer your habits. There is a trickle down effect of being healthy. It will help your mood and state of mind, which in turn can help you be a better spouse, parent and co-worker. A lot depends on your health and a lot of things can improve if you go for it!

3. DEDICATION TO YOUR **FAMILY**

Your family is a very important part of your life; try to keep them as close as possible. Make them a priority and treasure the gift that they are. Family is rarely easy or simple; they can be hard on us or hard to communicate with. If you are struggling with addiction or any bad habit, then they might not know how to talk to you or encourage you or help you. They mean well, but remember that they aren't necessarily professional counselors or doctors so give them the benefit of the doubt when they don't react the way you want them to. We are responsible and accountable for how we lead and love our family. We belong to them and they belong to us, so we ought to do the best we can. In this world we are all family. Some people don't have a blood family, but that doesn't mean you can't be family. Act as if everyone is family. Show compassion, all of us need it at some time in our lives.

4. INVEST IN WORK OR **SERVICE**, JOB OR CAREER

When you get the first three in the right order, I believe the fourth one will take care of itself. Be patient, you will find your true career, a life that God has planned for you. Investing in work can mean a couple of things. It can mean putting the time and hard work into it so that you feel a sense of pride and ownership in what you do. It can mean learning and growing as an employee so that more opportunities and promotions can be available for you. If you work but don't have a lot of love or passion for it, then you can use this time to be thankful that you have a job that provides for you and invest in yourself with education or training so that you can pivot into another job that holds more of your passions and interests. Don't look at work as an obstacle, try and see it as an opportunity.

I put this list into what I think is the proper order of what is most important. When I was drinking all the time alcohol became my number one and my other areas all suffered from not being in their proper place. In fact, I was killing myself slowly and the poison trickles down and impacts everything else. My family was being hurt because they weren't getting the best of me; in fact, they weren't getting the real me. My career and company was on life support. Now, when I wake up the first thing I do is pray to God, Jesus, and even Mary sometimes. I thank Him! He is my first. I go downstairs and get my cabbage juice. My health is second. Then I tell my girls and my wife good morning and spend the morning with them. Finally, after all that I go on with my work knowing that I have my day in order and God will guide me through it. Sure, all days aren't going to be perfect but my attitude toward it is much better. I'm much more positive now.

Picture this, your destination in life is kind of like a sailboat leaving port. The direction I was headed while I was drinking was treacherous; it would take me to a place where I would end up alone, broken, in poor health and very depressed. If I can just turn the steering wheel a little bit at a time, then I can end up headed in a much better direction; it would lead me to good faith, good health and better relationships with my family.

You see it's the little changes that over a period of time will lead your sailboat in a completely different direction. By changing your GPS heading by 1% you end up successful and healthy with a great family. Might not seem like much in the beginning but after a month of sailing the open sea that one percent change will help your boat find its way to where you were always meant to go. You won't have to swim or sail against the currents anymore because your discipline and faith will help you along the way! Our God will be pleased and can help make your waters smooth. He can send a breeze that will put wind in your sails and help push you farther than you thought you could go. Peace will come, like a gentle breeze, from a place that I really can't explain. I've felt the riptides and undercurrents that toss and drown your life. I've been in some of the stormiest waters that life has to offer. Heavenly tailwinds are better.

I know this may sound weird but, in a way, I actually feel like I have been drinking a little bit. I haven't had a drop of alcohol in over a week but I've felt some strange buzzed feeling. Not sure how to explain it, but I think I just might be getting the same feelings from being sober that I was from being buzzed, only without the calories. Now if I can get the flavor and experience for eating ice cream without the calories then I would be in Heaven. But then again what would Heaven be without ice cream?

CHAPTER FIVE

WHAT IS YOUR GRADE?

Today I was driving when I came up with this! What if I could grade myself on my recipe for a successful life? What if I could measure how I'm doing in all four areas and compare it to different parts of my life to see how I'm growing? I think this is a great idea and I want to challenge you to do it with me.

There are four areas (faith, health, family and career or service) and we can score ourselves on a 1-10 scale—1 being the lowest and 10 being the highest.

We can do this self-assessment anytime and compare it to how we've felt before in order to see what has changed and make some course adjustments from there. So, let's try it!

FAITH

If you truly want to get better, I believe that you must have a relationship with God. You need prayer and spiritual perspective that your life matters to God and He has a better story to tell through you.

Your Score: _____

HEALTH

You have to start taking care of yourself. Your body is a temple that houses your soul and your thoughts, consider how well you are taking care of your body.

Your Score: _____

FAMILY

These are the most meaningful relationships in your life, how are you getting along with everyone? This can be a huge support when things are going well or an extra stress when things are going wrong.

Your Score: _____

CAREER OR SERVICE

How is your job going? This is often a place where we spend 40+ hours a week. This environment can lead to high levels of stress or satisfaction. It is worth investing in yourself through your career.

Your Score: _____

A = 40-30   B = 29-25   C = 24-20

D = 19-15   F = 14-0

Today's date: _____ Today's score: _____

Today's date: _____ Today's score: _____

There is always room for improvement, so don't be too discouraged or too content with your score. If I can be honest with you, if you scored a 38 or higher then you might be lying to yourself. It might be awkward but if you have a trusted friend or mentor that you talk too often, you could consider asking them what they think your score might be, just to get some outside perspective on things. Either way, believe that there are lots of ways to improve your scores. Here are some examples I came up with for you to think about:

FAITH

You can start your day off with prayer each morning. Look for opportunities to pray throughout the day like driving in the car or while at work. Find things to thank God for throughout the day like your meal, your job, your family etc. Attend church and get involved there. Embark on spiritual disciplines like Bible reading, tithing, and journaling.

HEALTH

I can't say that cabbage juice tastes amazing but I'd challenge you to consider trying it. Start your morning off with something healthy. Start a workout routine: walking, jogging, sit ups, yoga, going to the gym, etc. I have taken my blood pressure and used that as a measurement for my health as well. Take the advice of your doctor into consideration. Drink lots of water. Gets the proper amount of sleep.

FAMILY

Invite your family into your faith journey, go to church together and take opportunities to pray together. Invite your family into your health journey as well. You can enjoy activities together, share healthy eating habits and actually sit down to eat the meals together. Take opportunities to talk and share how everyone is feeling. Find some special activities like movie nights, game nights, going out for a meal, or any kind of spontaneous adventure.

CAREER OR SERVICE

Write down some goals for your career over the next six months, year and five years. Concentrate on things that you could improve on or areas of your job where you can grow. What skills or abilities can you add to your resume to help you take your next step?

Your score can change at any time in either direction. I feel great about things today, I'd give myself a score of 30. Looking back to a few weeks ago I'd guess that my score back then was around 16. Cutting out alcohol made a pretty big and immediate improvement in my score. Of course it did!

CHAPTER SIX

THE CAPTAIN

By now I pray that you have the hopeful feeling that you can turn things around. No matter how you felt before, what you've struggled with, or what you score has been—you can get better! However, I can also insist that you won't see any growth or improvements if you don't really want it. You truly need to be sick and tired of being sick and tired. That can actually be a helpful state of mind, a place where you know that you don't want to fall any further and therefore you will start to climb back up. No one wants to hit the bottom. Most of us don't set goals to fall flat on our face, but it is from this position that we must find the courage and the drive to push forward. So find the hope that you can turn things around and firmly set your feet and heart to stand back up.

A buddy of mine started rehab with a great organization called "TN24", this stands for "THE NEXT 24 Hours." Its sounds like he is doing really well! He is feeling good and improving himself with the help of this organization.

I love this group's name. When you get down to it, all you and I have to do is really take care of the next 24 hours, one day at a time. The single days will blend together and over a period of time you and I will have completely changed our lives. Our ship will sail one day at a time, in the right direction and lead us towards a better destination. So many great leaders have shared that those daily habits were the catalysts to what led them to great success. It is the day-by-day force, applied over long periods of time that creates the best results.

It's funny; I use to look forward to the weekends because that is when the real partying or drinking really got going for me and all my friends. Now, all my weekends are consumed with my family and healthier stuff. Tennis lessons for our daughters, golf, yoga class, spearfishing and of course church every Sunday. Those are habitual changes that reflect not only my renewed commitment to my own health but also to my family's health. You can't predict what tomorrow will bring, but you can choose what direction to take. Come up with a process for how you want to choose your daily direction. You have to want that daily direction because nothing stays the same and new challenges and opportunities come as unending waves.

In life, hardly anything goes exactly as planned. There will always be someone or something that will throw a curveball at you. Simply take a step back and take a breath. See this challenge as a learning experience, then swing away. Make an adjustment and let that be your decision. You may not see the curveball coming, you probably didn't ask for it, but you can control the daily decision as you embrace the chaos and stand firm in your direction.

Here is where I am currently standing, right now I am sober and doing well. This is a place where I haven't been in a long time. This place is so much better than where I was. So, what does God have in store for you? What does He have in the future for you, your family, your kids and your grandkids? I don't really know everything that is on the horizon, but I have to say I'm pretty excited about it. I put a new captain on my sailboat, I call him Jesus Christ. You might have heard of him, He and the Easter Bunny are pretty popular this time of year. There were lots of reasons for me to surrender my life to Jesus and place Him as the captain of my life, but one particular reason is because of the way that He has mastered the water. Jesus slept through storms that made grown men cry. He walked on the water, putting it under His feet. He calmly spoke to a raging sea, commanding it to be still… and it obeyed Him. Raising people from the dead was also just as impressive. I knew that all of these things would come in handy as I journey through the seas of life, and I know that Jesus will help lead me in my daily decisions and in my reactions to sudden waves and storms.

You and I are forgiven; get over whatever it is that is holding you back from moving on. Today is a new day, your next 24 hours begins right now. Make a pledge, prayer and pact. Call it whatever you want, but make a decision today. There will be curveballs; change always brings waves, so keep your focus forward. It's like looking out through the windshield of your car, you can focus on the big picture in front of you or the small mirror to focus on what is behind you. You can't drive forward if your focus is on the mirror; you have to set your eyes to what is ahead of you. There are always appropriate times to look back and learn, but please don't try to drive forward while looking back.

Let's think about that question one more time. What does God have in store for you and your future? Who is the captain of your life? What changes do you want to see? Who are people that can come along side of you to support and encourage you? Don't be afraid to continue asking yourself those questions, even if some of them seem corny. Just think about it, what could you gain by having Jesus in your life? If you are reading through this with someone else in mind, what would you tell him or her about Jesus? What could He do for that person?

Here is another way to address the direction we are heading in life. What are the happiest people in life doing? I think that they must have found happiness from somewhere or something and then invested into that thing in their life. What about the saddest people? Where does their sadness or depression come from? I recently played golf with a friend who is going through a rough time in his life. He mentioned that he is depressed because he doesn't know where to go or what to do next. This guy is very wealthy, money isn't a concern, but it obviously isn't a source of joy either. It is easy for us to assume that material things bring joy, we are sold that idea in every commercial on the television and radio, but I think it is becoming more and more evident that happiness doesn't come with a price tag.

Many of us know that a broken marriage is a huge source of sadness, no matter how nice our house is or how good our bank account looks. I've seen friends go through this and I have gone through it myself. I was married once before and things didn't work out. My ex-wife left me for another man. A friend of mine was on the other side of this trouble; he was seeing another woman and cheating on his wife. These third wheels are cancerous to our soul and obviously to our marriage. We talked and he said something that really hit home with me. He said, "I couldn't keep the other relationship going because my soul just didn't feel right, so I ended it." He had decided to make things right with his wife and abandon the cancer that he invited into their marriage. I have never cheated on my wife with another person. I feel like I could never do that but I am shocked how many people I have met that have been cheated on or have cheated on their spouse. However, I have invited a cancer into my life and my home; I had a 30 year affair with alcohol and I got to the point where my soul didn't feel right either.

God wants what is best for us and He knows what is best for us. Being faithful to your spouse isn't a boring commandment meant to hinder your ability to enjoy your life, it is a blessing meant to enrich your life. The same goes for being sober, being honest, being humble, saying you're sorry and forgiving other people. When God commands these things He is giving us instructions on how to live our best life. The devil will try to influence you by lying and insisting that we should do what we want, what we feel will make us happy by living only for ourselves. My friend said that cheating on his wife made him happy and feel good for a time, but the cost caught up to him. Alcohol makes me feel good for a moment, but it comes with a cost.

Invest in things that bring true and lasting happiness. Marriage is meant to complement and enrich your life. Parenting is an opportunity to bless your life through your children. Work is a gift that can bring satisfaction and providence to your home. Health impacts your general well-being and state of mind. And your faith gives you grand perspective on what comes in this life and the next. All of these things are covered in your score from the last chapter, because all of these things are avenues of blessing for your life. I believe that you will find that happy people invest in these areas and sad people chase the wrong things that ultimately invite chaos into these areas. You can trust that God has your best interests in mind. If you aren't sure then I'd like you to try investing in these areas. Bring up your score in all four areas and see how you feel.

I'm about to go to bed. I no longer use alcohol to help me sleep; I am drinking tea and taking melatonin instead. This is a daily decision to change the way I prepare for sleep. I know that investing in a good night of sleep will bring me a greater opportunity for a good day tomorrow. One day at a time, one decision at a time, investing in what is good for me. Jesus take the wheel.

CHAPTER SEVEN

MISSION STATEMENT

Have you ever heard this phrase before: "If you fail to plan, then you plan to fail?" I've heard another phrase from a friend of mine, "It's better to create than to react." I love that statement; I even wrote it down in the front of my Bible. Both of these statements speak to the importance of being proactive with your life. You have to be prepared for the life that you want to have. Too often we simply react to what is going on around us and we miss new opportunities and blessings that fly by us. In the last chapter, we thought about the kind of future and life that we want to experience. The next step is actually writing it out. Put pen to paper and take a firm stance on where you want to go and who you want to be!

Again, if you haven't already, take some time to find some ideas. Pray to God, find a happy place, and talk to a mentor or trusted friend. Do what you need to do. This is not an easy assignment but you and I both need to have a mission statement. It is an important next step. This can be fun! We are meant to dream, to envision a brighter future and to cling to things that are good. Getting clean, building stronger relationships with family members, getting out of debt, increasing education, sobriety, losing weight—these are all great goals to focus our mission around.

If you don't have a mission, then you are just a ship without a rudder. I don't know if you read the Bible, but please consider this passage for a moment and how it could impact your life.

If you need wisdom, ask our generous God, and He will give it to you.
He will not rebuke you for asking. But when you ask Him,
be sure that your faith is in God alone.
Do not waiver, for a person with divided loyalty is as
unsettled as a wave of the sea that is blown and tossed by the wind...
they are unstable in everything they do.
James 1:5-8 NLT

If you lack faith and direction, then I encourage you to go to God to get some. I know I have benefited from talking to priests and pastors in the past. That may be something that you would consider. There are also great resources available on mentorship that help identify an individual's next step, check out a book called "MentorU".

Let's try writing some thoughts down as we shape our mission statement. These questions might map out a destination for your mission statement.

YOUR DESTINATION

1. What hobbies do you really enjoy? _____

_____

_____

2. What can you do to help promote a healthy lifestyle? _____

_____

_____

3. What are things you do for other people that make you feel good?

_____

_____

4. If you knew you couldn't fail at anything you tried, what would you do?

_____

_____

5. What defining characteristics do you want to have? _____

_____

_____

MISSION STATEMENT

My name is _____ and I want to experience _____

_____

_____ in my life.

I want to do _____

_____ in my life.

And I want to be known for _____

_____ in my life.

I hope that was enough room to write. Either way, I encourage you to write and save your mission statement in a journal or on your computer where you can easily access it in the future. You can, and should, tweak your mission statement as you go through life. But now you have a destination, a direction and a heading for your life. It will be easier to identify good days when you feel you are headed in the right direction. It will be easier to weather bad days when you know that where you are going, is better than where you are. I know it's a journey we all have to take but with the right focus and a plan, your life can be great! Every day is a new day. Every moment brings a new opportunity.

April 18th, 2017

22 days sober

It is Day 22! This is a day that I have been waiting for and praying for. I've found some resources that say it takes 22 days to start a new habit. So, I have been sober for 22 days. It has been three weeks of drinking cabbage juice, making healthier choices, and investing into things that actually matter to me. At the same time, three weeks isn't long enough for me to forget exactly how awful I felt throwing up, shaking and shivering through withdrawals. I knew that I needed to make some changes and I believed that these new habits would work. My sister has been checking in on me, wanting to know how my journey is going. I can confidently tell her that I'm doing really well. Once my desperation to not be sick finally found inspiration on how to build healthier habits, it started coming together.

There was a group of friends who went out fishing on the Gulf of Mexico during the summer. They went out on a little boat and traveled miles out into the wide-open ocean. They picked a spot and dropped their lines. The little boat rocked and bounced over the rolling waves. It didn't take long for one of the young men to experience the sensation of seasickness. Moments later, the poor kid was tossing his breakfast over the side of the boat. It was a miserable time.

Imagine feeling stuck, anchored to the bottom of the ocean while tossing in the chaos at the top. Hours went by, but they felt like days. The passion and excitement for the trip was now fully replaced by frustration and helplessness. When the time came to head back, the anchor came up and the boat began to travel back to shore. The boat flew off the waves and crashed back into the water as they sped back home. Oddly enough, the seasickness completely disappeared the moment that the boat started moving toward the shore. There is something about encountering the reckless waves while being still that creates the miserable nausea. Don't allow yourself to be anchored in chaos and despair. It came together for me when I finally realized that things will never get better unless I cut ties with where I am and begin to move forward.

It will come together for you too! What are you desperate to change? What inspires you to change? Are you ready to commit to the process? If you are still searching for those answers, then keep searching until you find them. Don't give up! Once you see things clearly, life will be more full of fun and hope. The best years of your life are on their way. Try not to be stressed through these questions. That won't help you find answers. Go for a run or walk, get out of your normal space and find a space where you can search your heart and pray for guidance. Take the opportunity to change and grow seriously, but don't allow that pressure to create more despair in your heart. Honestly, in my experience, I knew what I needed to do for a long time; getting started was really the issue. I think that I knew for many years, but I needed the desperation, inspiration, and the dedication to come together all at once. I wish I had started earlier, and I hope you start as soon as possible.

If you are like me and you struggle with drinking, I hope you've started your journey. I hope you wrote out a mission statement and have found some inspiration on what steps to take next. It doesn't matter what your struggle may be, you need to start your march against it. I know that my journey is far from over, this is just the beginning, but today is a milestone for me. If I can make it this far, I can make it! Even if I fall, I can get back up and try again. It takes desperation to get better, with an inspiration on how to do it, and finally you need the dedication to walk through it. I thank God that I am not where I was, He has guided me this far and the place I'm at today is better than where I was 22 days ago. I guess that is the best thing we can ever hope for, that today can be better than yesterday and tomorrow can be better than today. I don't want to spend much more time bragging on my 22 days, I know that God has put the wind in my sails to get here; I just want to encourage and challenge you to believe that you can take real steps towards your mission. You can do this!

May 1st, 2017

Well, I missed writing a few times this past week. Nothing has really changed. I am making my daily decisions and staying committed to them. One thing that has changed is my juice formula: 12oz of spring water, about one cup of red cabbage, one green apple, half of a banana, four or five ice cubes, and one packet of Stevia. This tastes pretty good and is definitely my favorite recipe at this point. I encourage you to try it and maybe find a way to send me your thoughts or suggestions on how to improve it more. The juice can act like a meal replacement but I usually still eat something with it. Each morning I have either a protein bar or a few eggs with toast. In my opinion, this part of my daily routine is not that complicated or hard for anyone to replicate. You don't have to copy me in any way; I'm just saying that the decision to eat a decent breakfast isn't that difficult. This is a basic decision that anyone can make.

It is all about the basics. I don't believe that we are necessarily born into our struggles; we give in to them. We may have certain things that we are more naturally prone to struggle with, but ultimately our actions and responses are our responsibility. I know people who say that their parents drank, smoked, or ate unhealthy so they were raised to do the same. I understand where they are coming from. That is a struggle in every sense, but there has to be a point where your actions are your own and you have to decide to break old patterns and start new ones. If it is a family thing, then you may have to be the first person to break off and start a new habit or tradition. Someone has to be the first to be sober, finish school, make the marriage work, break free from debt or eat healthy. Why not you? Why not now? The things of your past can feel like anchors that hold you down, cut loose from those burdens and allow yourself to be free. Start making the right decisions and soon you'll feel some momentum, the wind will catch your sails and your movement will feel easier and more natural.

I believe that we can make it. Even if we fail, we know that we are trying. Anything is better than staying still.

CHAPTER EIGHT
FAILING UPWARDS

May 8th, 2017

This entry was not written today, but today was a significant day for me. On this day, I reached 42 consecutive days of sobriety. I am proud of those 42 days. I learned a lot and I wrote the previous chapters of my story about what I learned. However, today is also the day when I started drinking again.

May 29th, 2017

The past three weeks have taken a toll on my family. I slowly started to drink again. My wife and friends didn't know at first. Then I started drinking a little more, getting drunk just before bed. I could see that my wife and family members were mad and worried about me once again. My life got worse very quickly. My health got worse and my back account was rapidly emptying. I became weaker and weaker as I drank more and more. I just wanted to relax. I just wanted to drink.

My most unattractive traits were coming back out and my wife's patience with me was wearing dangerously thin. Yesterday, she seemed completely done. I had pissed people off, proven people right, and let a lot of people down. I am afraid that I've ruined things with my wife for good this time. I felt depressed, and I hated seeing people see me this way again. I had to get sober. I had to try.

I don't know what your thoughts are reading of my falling off the wagon. I can't tell you what to think, but I can continue to share my thoughts and experiences with you. I don't think that I've lost perspective on my 42 days of sobriety, I don't think that I've lost any of the truths that I've found and shared in these earlier chapters of my story. If anything, I believe that they are truer and more important now than I did before. I have fallen and I have failed. In doing so, I've hurt people and hurt myself. I've also gained some new perspectives. I've gained an opportunity to test and improve some methods. And I can only hope and pray that my insufficiencies point out my need and dependence for a merciful friend in Jesus. I've now fallen, and I can't take that back or make it go away. However, in this place where I now stand, I must choose to fall forward.

I lost my focus and my ship got caught in a riptide. I can choose to give up completely and be swept away to sea, or I can refocus my attention to the future again, to the place that I want to be. There aren't any other options than that. Falling forward means taking what I've learned and trying my best to use it for good. I hope my wife understands that I want to use this for good; I didn't mean to frustrate her. I hope she understands that. This might not be the only time I fall back into drinking, so I can't afford to not have learned something from this. I can learn from the choice to drink again, how it made others feel, how it made me feel, and maybe address some of the break downs that led me back to alcohol.

I have to go through detox once again. This time I have a plan and some experience, but of course there is now a little bit of curiosity in my mind that maybe I can do things better this time. My stomach was in pain again. The cold sweats are back and my heart is racing. I told my wife that I actually forgot how much I hate detoxing. She replied, "I don't know why you do it." She was referring to me drinking again. I will start the cabbage juice once again, but this time I'm starting with my best recipe. I also didn't stop drinking completely, I had a little bit to drink and plan on cutting it completely as I go forward.

May 31st, 2017

I had cold sweats all night on the first day. I told my wife to feel my body and she said, "Yuck!" Now that is something that no one wants to hear from their spouse. I was sweating a lot but I didn't feel so terrible. I got up a few times to drink some water throughout the night, and then I'd go back to bed and just sweat. The next day, I relied on my cabbage juice and I'm feeling much better! I think that it is definitely possible to detox in two days and that it really works.

Today is day three and I feel great and I'm looking forward to doing some landscaping work and drinking my cabbage juice. I'm going to make coffee for my wife as soon as I am done writing.

I'm still concerned about my marriage. I know that God has a plan and I'm going to trust in Him. I will always remember this crazy journey that I've put myself through. It isn't easy; in fact, it is really hard. I felt like I was I was going through Hell. Now I just pray that I don't have to go through the hell of facing another divorce. My wife is a great person. I pray that she sees changes in me and will believe in me, that our love will be stronger than ever. I can only hope and pray. But I know it will take time and a lot of patience.

June 1st, 2017

I honestly thought that I would be done with this book by now, but here I am at 4:13am. There is still much to learn and I have more thoughts to share. Here are a few thoughts that I'm having this morning, maybe these will make sense to you. First, I know that some people can drink socially and be totally fine. There are possibly many readers who don't struggle with alcohol or any kind of substance abuse, for you it is something completely different. Jesus drank alcohol; it may be different than a White Claw or vodka but there was alcohol involved in the wine that he made and drank at that wedding. Moderation is a real and tangible lifestyle for many people, they don't constantly push the limits on how much or how often they drink.

Second, I believe there are people like me who are just drawn to alcohol at a greater level. We need to be very careful that alcohol doesn't take a hold of us. We should be aware of its influence on us and our attraction to it. It could be a matter of chemistry or psychology that draws us to it. Either way, we have to acknowledge this and understand that this isn't some lighthearted struggle for us. This is a serious battle going on and we need to be aware of not only how alcohol influences us, but also how outside influencers pull us to drink. There are tailwinds and riptides, forces that carry us to safety and forces that pull us out to treacherous seas.

My third thought goes more into the influencers that are all around us. The reason why it is important to acknowledge the severity of our struggle is the severe number of influencers in the world around us. There are powerful forces at play, inside and outside of our heart and mind. We can't walk through life oblivious to the attractions and distractions that are constantly thrown at us. Think about how many commercials for beer there are on the television and radio. We hear other people talk about it and promote it. There are also things like fear, anxiety, and discouragement that make drinking feel like an escape. I think that I know this is a trap but let me just share how I have felt about this at times in my life.

I was in the habit of drinking for decades. I would come home from work with some beer and hear all about how awful it is that I went out for more beer. For me, the nagging and the judgment only made me want to drink and withdraw more into my escape hatch. In some of those times, I felt like the friends and family members who bitched at me for drinking didn't really want me to get better, they just wanted to judge me. My other response, besides drinking more, was to try and hide it from my friends and family. I didn't want to hear it from them, so I tried my best to conceal how much and how often I drank. This only further isolated me from other people and pushed me to drink more.

That was how I would feel sometimes. I know that I can't let other people's perception, or criticism, drive me to drink more. I can't afford to let other people influence my behavior. I won't judge them and I can't let them judge me. There is only one person who can judge me and His name is God. You and I aren't qualified to judge each other. The Holy Spirit can lead us to the truth, and we can find help to see things through. I know that I struggle with alcohol and I want to rely on God to judge me and hope that I can rely on friends and family to support me through it. I just hope that I haven't lost them already.

Have you ever thought about it? What makes you want to drink more? Is it an escape hatch to hide away from feelings you have buried deep inside you? Is it simply a chemical dependency that you've built up? There has to be more than just the taste or smell, more than just the design on a bottle. Something is pulling us in, and the faster we figure out what those influences are the faster we can make a plan to effectively fight against them.

My wife and I haven't found a healthy way to talk about it. Again, I've always felt judged for my struggle. I know that I need to get better and the things I've been told aren't necessarily untrue—except for some of the meaner comments—but I wish we could talk about it in a more productive manner. I think starting earlier would have helped. I think talking about it with a professional would have helped. Maybe those thoughts would be helpful for you.

CHAPTER NINE
ROCK BOTTOM

July 8th, 2018

Well, it has been a year since I last wrote in this book. I just turned 49 years old, I've been dry for 9 days this time, and I am feeling good. I went through withdrawals last week, exercising my two-day detox method. I still believe in that process, my process of cleansing my system and starting my sobriety. The process of staying away from alcohol is less inspiring at the moment. Over the past year, I've had more and more opportunities to use my two-day detox process. We may have a problem here.

I'm glad that I started writing this book over a year and a half ago. Through this process, I've experienced the tide of drawing in to sobriety and then pulling back out away from it. The forces that pull me seem to be pulling extra hard, and I've let them get a hold of me once again. One of the things that encourages me is reading back through what I've written so far, to see victories—although short lived—and to believe that it is possible for me to get where I want to be. I hope you haven't given up on me yet. I haven't given up on you or myself; I still believe that we can figure this out. This isn't easy, I think we both know that, but that doesn't mean we shouldn't try.

December 22, 2018

Let me recap some of July and August for you just so we stay caught up on my life and my journey. The month of July came and went with some moments of celebration and victory. I had my 49th birthday and we celebrated our 9th wedding anniversary. My wife and I had somehow made it another year. I'm so glad that we did. I had some weeks that were alcohol-free, but I also had some days that weren't. It wasn't the best month ever but it certainly wasn't the worst. I didn't know it at the time but the worst was yet to come.

Along came the month of August, and we took a family trip to Clearwater Beach. One of my daughters turned 21 years old. That age brings me back to some crazy times. Back in the "old days", we didn't have cell phones, we would have to call friends and meet up somewhere. We did have beepers; those were pretty great. If you are reading this and you don't know what a beeper is, then stop what you are doing and look it up. Beepers were basically a little square devices that most people wore on their belt or had in their purse. Someone would call it and leave number for you to call back; it was sort of like texting but all you got was the number for the person who was trying to reach you. Just believe this; you were cool if you had a beeper. Life was certainly different back then, but somewhere in the middle of that time in my life I began this toxic relationship with a toxic substance.

It has been such a long time. If you haven't realized this already, then you need to know that life can slip by you so fast. You can turn 21 years old, have your whole life in front of you, and then suddenly you are looking back at this time decades later. No matter how old you are today, imagine looking forward to the next ten years, what do you hope to see? Now imagine being ten years older and looking back at your life, you probably have the same dream for what you'd like to see. The truth is that those two visions won't line up if you can't figure out your mission statement and find a way to make it work. I'm about to close the door on my forties, so I want to spend my fifties in a much happier and healthier state of life. I want to make some memories that I can look back on for the rest of my life and be proud of.

Again, I have hope for you and for me. We can find the mission that is worth living and we can live it out. I'm writing this after hitting rock bottom, I haven't shared that story just yet but trust me when I say that hope and grace are still available to us. God, our Heavenly Father, is for us and wants to see us do our best. He is in charge of my life, even though I've failed Him so many times. He knew what He was getting into when He called me to be His follower, and yet He called me anyway. You and I are not called to believe or follow God because of how good we are, but because God sees something better in us than we can see in ourselves. We will always tell a better story with Him in our life than without Him. It is almost Christmas now, and my gift is to still be here today to continue telling my story and continue writing this book. I hit rock bottom in

September, but God got me through it.

September 15th, 2018

I was drunk. Actually, I was more than drunk; I was drinking myself to death. I had way too much to drink and I knew that I was in trouble. I called my sister's friend who was in Alcoholics Anonymous. Thank God, he came and got me less than seven minutes after I called him. I had been feeling alone, depressed, and was obviously drinking heavily. I know now that I wasn't alone, there were angels watching out for me. God had sent me a person who gave me some hope, a light to hold onto in my dark moment. That was all I needed to get through this and God knew that. God can throw you a life vest in a situation where it feels like you are drowning.

I was at rock bottom; the only lower I could be was dead. I had poisoned my body with the substance that I had been fighting for quite some time now. Looking back I know that this was the bottom and I had to move up from here, if I could just make it through the night. I got into the car and we got out of there.

He asked how I was doing and I tried to communicate in my mental state and how much I had to drink. After listening to me, he called a few of his friends that could get me to a place that would help me out. I was ready to give up but he had some ideas. He figured that the hospital would be the safest place to treat my physical and emotional needs. So getting admitted into the hospital was our mission. It didn't take long to get there and we went in. The nurse said that they wouldn't accept me and there wasn't anything that they could do for me. So, we drove to another hospital and they said the same thing.

There was another option; I would have to Baker Act myself. I told the nurse that I was fearful that I might kill myself. It was Saturday, September 15th, and I was taken into the Baker Act section of the hospital. I spent my first day and 20 hours here, constantly throwing up and going number two. Both of these actions burned, I believe that it was all of the acid leaving my body. After those painful first hours, I was checked out of the hospital and sent to Psychiatric Hospital. I started in a holding area for the first four hours, still shitting out the poison that I had put into my body. They finally processed all of my information and I was officially checked in to the facility.

I was placed into a room with a roommate. They took my shoe laces and I was basically wearing nothing but a hospital gown. This is when I started to go through the alcohol withdrawals again. It was miserable going through these familiar pains and aches, this time I was in an unfamiliar place with unfamiliar people. I had to go through this detox under medical supervision. My recovery was very organized and scheduled, from the time you get up to the time you go to bed. There is definitely a benefit to having the medical professional side of recovery, but you have to trust and comply with what they ask of you. There isn't a lot of pride in being admitted to a facility like this, and it isn't the kind of place that you want to stay longer than you need to.

I found out that I was one of two patients being treated for alcohol detox. Most of the other patients were dealing with severe mental traumas and disorders. Take my roommate for example. He would scream at the top of his lungs for most of the night; it felt like he had some kind of demon inside of him that was trying to get out. Needless to say, sleep was hard to come by. As I stayed up listening to my roommate scream, I actually tried saying the Lord's Prayer over and over again to calm the situation and myself. I know that people deal with real medical and chemical conditions; I just never expected to find myself kept in the company of mentally unstable people. I knew that it was my fault that I was here, but did I like being where I was? Hell no!

I simply told the truth to the staff, that I wasn't recovering while listening to my roommate scream all night and they allowed me to change rooms. This job must be hard, but at the same time I wasn't that impressed or encouraged by the staff at this facility. They definitely did what needed to be done, and safety was never a question. I just wonder why they don't make more of an effort to personally connect with patients or why the facility doesn't look for more ways to provide encouragement or educational resources for patients. I suspect that it's because of the mental state of patients in a psych ward; you might not be able to have sincere conversations or teachable moments. I know that I'm a patient just the same, but I knew that I didn't belong here. I needed to do what was necessary and follow the steps for recovery.

One time of day that wasn't so bad was lunchtime and arts and crafts. Surprisingly, the food wasn't that bad. I noticed that everyone looked forward to lunch; it was mutually the best part of each day. I used that time to try and connect a little to other patients, anyone besides my screaming roommate. I walked around and found a guy that looked pretty normal. It turned out he was the other patient in this facility who was going through alcohol detox just like me. It was good to connect with someone and have a shared experience. It felt like another small way that God was keeping me above water. And then I really found something special. There was a donated book called, 2 Chairs : The Secret That Changes Everything, and this was a game changer for me. The premise of the book centers on spending time to talk with God, to talk and to listen. So, I rebooted my habit of prayer while going through hell. This book, which was donated to the facility, somehow found its way into my hands and it gave me hope.

In the Bible, there are a lot of letters that were written from inside of a prison. The Apostle Paul famously wrote some of the most quoted pieces of the New Testament while under arrest. This psychiatric hospital is the closest I want to be to prison, but like Paul I need to find a greater purpose in the place I am in. Tough times can actually force you to dig deeper and get a firmer grasp on what you believe and what you need. You shouldn't literally throw yourself off a building in hopes of learning to fly, but if you do find yourself falling then you better find it in yourself to fly or find someone to catch you. In this moment, I need to rediscover that God will catch me and learn how to stop falling.

December 27th, 2018

I have to wonder what is going through the mind of the reader at this point. What is going on your mind right now? You don't have to tell me, but maybe you should write it down somewhere. You might be thinking about my story, but I think you could be thinking about your own life. Maybe you have been where I've been, and you are afraid of going back.

Perhaps you have never been where I've been, but you are afraid that you might be headed there. My hope is that this story does evoke some kind of response from you, especially if it leads you to make a positive change. I know that my life has changed a lot since this part of my story. That journey lasted for four days, three of them in that psych ward.

Today, around 100 days later, I am enjoying my morning at home with my cat, Skippy Lou. This is a great start to my day, writing and petting the cat. This book has become as much of my journey as anything else. I don't know where or how it will end, but I am dedicated to finishing it. Not knowing where my story goes from here is almost freeing. It is a release of pressure to align the pieces of my life to fit perfectly the way I want them to. Things could get better; I could conquer my drinking habit, and publish a successful book. I know things could not go my way, but I shouldn't have to live in that fear. No matter what happens, I want to surrender everything into God's hands and just try to do my best with what I have. I've already walked through the fire, God saw me through it. So, I think that I can have hope for whatever comes next.

CHAPTER TEN

REALITY CHECK

I love listening to great speakers and storytellers. Anthony Robbins is someone that I especially like to listen to. He was telling a story and got into a great discussion on goals and dreams. He explained that there are times when dreams are simply just that, a dream. However, there comes a day when you look back at that dream and find that it has become a present reality. He insists that for many of us, the dream of the future was actually more exciting and captivating than the accomplishment itself. There is a temptation to stop dreaming once you have achieved something, and people who do that lose a lot of excitement in their life. So, as Anthony would say, we have to let the journey of chasing dreams become our destination. We have to love the process that we are in. We should always have a dream to chase, a magical sense that things could be better, and an anticipation that the journey will bring us to growth and adventure.

So today, while I was in yoga class, I started thinking about some past and present goals that we've had in our family. For one, the yoga studio we are in is our studio. Nine months ago it was just an idea. That idea turned into a goal of ours and is now a reality. We began to believe in it, wrote down some goals, and then gave it the attention that it needed. Our studio is called *Yoga 4 Fitness* and it has been growing and helping people become healthier.

To date, we have 125 members enrolled in our yoga studio. We are proud of the progress that our start up made, and we want to continue dreaming and enjoying the process of growing this business. I know that I have more to give, especially since some of my worst drinking has taken place around the beginning of this business' life. So the future of this business can trend up as I have more and more to offer my wife in helping make this thing grow.

I am excited to share that I have been sober for about four months now! This is a major accomplishment and I am more hopeful now than ever that I can continue this journey. I'm still finding my way, but I want to enjoy this journey and find new excitement and inspiration along the way. The destination is to be in a continual process of growth, a continual process of health, and a continual process of sobriety. My current daily routine is to get up around 5am-6am in the morning. I pray and get my breakfast going, get the kids ready to school and then drive them there. After I get back to the house I make sure that I have all of my things ready for the day ahead. I have a 40-45 minute drive time to work, and I use this time to listen to great and inspirational speakers like Joyce Meyers, Joel Osteen, and Tony Robbins. Sometimes I listen to the radio but only things that encourage me, so mostly country or Christian music. Lately, I have loved anything from the bands, *Mercy Me* and *King and Country*.

One day in the car, a *Mercy Me* song came on the radio and I felt overwhelmed by the Holy Spirit. It was so amazing; I had chills all over my body. I could feel something move in my body and tears just flowed out of my eyes. My goosebumps had goosebumps. I felt tremendous joy, a euphoric peace that I can't really explain. The music helped my soul connect to God, it really moved me and I felt God's presence in such a refreshing way. I'm going to call it a God-filled experience, a time of connection with the Holy Spirit. These experiences are so encouraging and come as reminders that we can look back on and remember that God is with us. Music has a way of helping us make those connections, and those morning drives are a great time to either hear encouraging words from a speaker or listening to music that truly touches my heart.

This routine has helped put some wind in my sails. It helps spur me into a productive day. Eating well, caring for my kids, listening to positive content are all things that propel me forward. I've identified those things and I understand why each of them helps me. I think it is important to find a helpful routine and also understand why each step is helpful. The "why" in this case is just as helpful as the "what". Those helpful steps become more real, more personal, when you know why you need to do them. You can better celebrate your routine when you better understand the heart behind your actions. I can do better and feel better about being a father and husband. I can be more prepared and be more proud about my work. Taking action is hard when you don't believe in it.

I think it is worth repeating that change doesn't happen overnight. It is an applied force over a long period of time. So do something, anything, to get started and don't be discouraged if you don't get there right away.

Let the small changes make a long lasting impact over time, a one-degree change doesn't seem like much at first but that change builds and builds to ultimately lead you to a completely new place. It can lead to a new life, a new reality, and a new you. Trust me, you will feel defeated if you look for any kind of immediate fix or remedy. Trust the process and let the journey be your destination. God has a plan for you and you can trust in His path. Everything we do, every choice and action, matters to God. We never stop mattering to God, and so what we do will always be important to Him. You don't graduate or retire out of significance. As long as you live and breathe, your life matters and your journey matters. So take a hold of your life and the direction that you are headed. Don't let yourself pretend that the journey doesn't matter. Every day must be accounted for, so choose wisely how you spend your days.

Coming out of my time in the psych ward, I knew that I was letting too much of my journey slip away from me. I had lost the sense of daily purpose. That is why I want to review this idea with you, so that we both don't forget that every day matters. Don't throw today away. Even if you failed yesterday; even if you failed for the 1,000th time; don't throw today away. Sometimes people lose hope in today; they don't believe that they have anything left to give or to fight for. They are wrong. If there were no purpose left then we wouldn't be here. Don't let fear or guilt take away the desire to live in God's purpose. Jesus died so that our sin would no longer hold us captive. Walk in grace and know that your life still matters, no matter what.

CHAPTER ELEVEN
FORGIVE, DON'T FORSAKE

January 27th, 2019

Remember when I said that I had hit rock bottom? Well, today is a new form of rock bottom. I am still sober, alcohol hasn't beaten me but it sure feels like life has. There have been lots of things that are hard to write about, but this is the hardest. I don't want to get into too many details, but I feel like I need to share this development in my life's story. I hope that writing this out provides some kind of help to me, to anyone involved, and to the readers. I thought things were getting better. They were fine, better than fine, actually. I am so confused; my heart doesn't know how to feel.

Around 2am I was struggling to sleep when I heard my daughters iPad alert that a call was coming in. The iPad is linked to my wife's phone and I could see the name of the man who was calling. I decided to wake up my wife and ask her about the call. She initially said that she didn't know why he was calling. I left our bedroom and went out to the couch; I knew something wasn't right.

Moments later, my wife came out of our room and joined me; she looked like she had just seen a ghost. I asked her what was going on but she sat in silence for a long time. Finally, she informed me that she has been involved with this other man, the man that has called in the middle of the night.

I don't know what to think or how to feel. I still love her; I can't help but feel like that is the right thing to feel. I believe that everything, no matter how bad, can bring goodness into our lives somehow. That has to be true, because life is full of so much bad and yet we still find so much goodness through it all. But that doesn't stop me from feeling hurt, angry, and confused at this moment. It is an impossible situation, but I know that nothing is really impossible if we are willing to work at it. I truly believe that evil forces are working their hardest to split up our family once and for all.

I know the pains and frustrations that I have brought into our home. I am not innocent of bringing an unwanted force into the marriage. I don't believe that my drinking is a legitimate excuse for being cheated on, but I understand how that stress and hurt drove a wedge between us. I want to forgive her for what she has done. I know that is the best thing for our family, especially for the kids. But I don't know if we should be together anymore, there are mutual hurts present now and it is a lot to handle for either of us. We have been married for over nine years, and a lot has happened in that time. There are so many memories and cherished moments, and there are many heart aches and speed bumps that we hit along the way. The hardest part is knowing that it only takes one of us to decide that this is all over, but it will take two of us to commit to making it work. What would you do?

GETTING DIVORCED

We are in the process of getting a divorce. At the moment, we are still married and living together. My heart is broken. So, I called a great Christian friend of mine and got some advice. He had been in a similar position and I knew that he could give me some insight. We talked for a while and he gave me some suggestions if I wanted to try and fix things. He said that he doesn't think that she actually wants to be with anyone else, that she made a bad decision and she may want to work things out. He suggested that I apologize to her, seek an apology from her, and then figure out if we both want to take each other back. Although I felt hurt, I still knew that my drinking had hurt her so I understood why I needed to apologize to her. I also understand that it will take both her and I together to make things work.

I want to make things work, so this will end up being her decision. All indications point to our eventual divorce in April 2019. I want to yell and blow up at her, but I know that wouldn't help either of us. Going off on her would essentially mean that I had given up on us and it might also make her go run into his arms again. So after a lot of thought and prayer, I asked her to choose between him and me. I told her it was her choice, not mine; I can't make her do anything. I told her that I can forgive her but she needs to make her choice quickly because I can't continue to live with her while she is still seeing this other man. I don't think that I deserve that.

So, she made a phone call and broke things off with him. We had gone to church together that Sunday morning and the sermon was on anger and guilt. Those are two things that are definitely at play here in our situation, for both of us.

This is really hitting me in ways I didn't expect. I am now realizing for the first time that my wife was angry with me and never really had opportunities to express how hurt she felt by my drinking. By the way she has acted, I have to guess that she has been holding on to some heavy resentment and pain. What I do know is that if she can't forgive me, then this simply won't work out. The same goes for me, if I don't forgive her. In my opinion, we both need to forgive ourselves. I need to release some guilt from my drinking and she needs to forgive herself for cheating on me. I believe that it will be hard to forgive someone else if you can't forgive yourself; it is hard to give something that you don't have inside of you. It is hard to be hopeful, or gracious, or forgiving to others when you won't allow any of that for yourself. I have God's grace inside of me, and by His grace I have been sober for nearly five months. I have felt change and hope, so I have to see that potential and hope in other people.

February 4th, 2019

Forgiveness will be the key to making things work out. I am praying harder than I've ever prayed to find forgiveness for her and from her. Like I said, our relationship is heading towards a divorce unless something changes. Anything is possible, but we aren't headed in the right direction quite yet. It has been over a week now and I have moved out of the house.

We still talk to each other every day, just to check in, and I've been helping out at the yoga studio. It is hard. Part of me wants to let her go and I don't feel great about trying to make things work. I am questioning myself and my hope for us is fading. I am still feeling confused about this situation and being away from my family is really difficult for me. It hurts feeling like I'm the only one being punished at the moment, but that is where we are at right now. Today, I'm just praying for patience and for help. I am putting God in charge and looking for Him to guide me through this season of life. I don't know if I should keep calling her, but I love her so much.

GOD WILL NEVER FORSAKE YOU

Let's look for some positives. In my process of health, I've lost 28 pounds and I'm in really good health. My faith is as strong as it has ever been; I'm talking to God every day and depending on Him for everything. My finances are being covered, although I will soon be sending more money to my wife (soon to be ex-wife). In all of these things, I feel God has not abandoned me or left me to fight these battles on my own. I am choosing to stay positive and even excited for some future opportunities. I've thought about starting another company, I might get into it more in the future.

My family life is obviously a mess. I recently received the divorce papers and it hit me really hard. I knew they were coming but them finally being here is hitting me harder than I expected. We have agreed on some terms for our life moving forward; my wife wants to give us three months to see if we should try again with our marriage or just move on from each other. It is odd to have that "trial" period while the divorce is scheduled and approaching on the calendar. I guess we are testing if we can make it work together and also testing if we can make things work apart. So, to practice a divorced lifestyle I am taking the girls with me over the weekend. I am happy to spend time with them but this isn't how I want things to be forever.

Nevertheless, I can't help but feel God's presence all around me. I actually cry tears of joy at times, feeling a kind of peace that is hard to explain. There are visions in my mind of things that I have prayed for but haven't been accomplished yet. It gives me so much hope and joy to feel like dreams and desires are still attainable. I have ideas that I believe God wants to bless me. There may be blessings coming my way. Going through a divorce makes you feel unwanted and alone, but God is helping me push those feelings away. This book is a gift to me, it is a space to work out and write reminders to myself about God's providence. I can already look back to some of the things that God has brought me through and I can have hope for the future. Sometimes, hope is all you need to keep you going. My world is not falling apart, it is falling into place. Falling hurts, but God can gently catch you and put you on your feet.

Imagine being on a sinking ship in the middle of the ocean. There is hopelessness and despair that sinks into your heart. Then there is a moment when you remember the lifeboat; these rafts exist in order to give you another chance to stay afloat when everything around you is sinking. I can't feel sorry for myself. I can hop into the lifeboat and give myself to the tides of God's will. I can breathe, move, and share my testimony of how God has not forsaken me. And He will not forsake you either.

FORGIVENESS

February 13th, 2019

    I am enjoying some more music from Casting Crowns, especially this song about just being held by God. I know that I have to let go of the hate and resentment that I am holding on to. It has been nearly three weeks of trying to adjust and process this weight in my life. I keep thinking of this other man and my anger towards him and towards my wife. If I'm being honest, focusing on him or them together is only making things worse. Focusing on the cause of my pain is not helping it heal, and I know that this focus and obsession is holding back my freedom to forgive. So while I am asking God for the blessings of peace and understanding, I am actively holding on to the burden that weighs me down. I think that we often say that we want to forgive someone but we struggle to actually let go of our anger and pain.

    That anger and pain is an anchor, a heavy weight, which prohibits us from moving forward to better and safer waters. There is a storm surging all around us, the waves are crushing and punishing us on all sides. We have dropped our anchor in this place and are now tied down to it. If we don't find a way to pull the weight up or cut it loose, then we will drown here. There is no way forward if we cannot release the weight that binds us down. Even a little bit of weight will hold you back. If you have ever jumped or fallen into water with your clothes on (especially your shoes) then you know that you can't move freely or confidently. Even those little weights matter. Some of us have held onto weights for a long time, and the discomfort has become normal. You can convince yourself that it isn't affecting you, but considering my marriage and how the burden of anger and pain eroded our relationship.

February 15th, 2019

I didn't get into writing yesterday. Valentine's Day definitely brought a rollercoaster of emotions. I did enjoy taking my daughters out to dinner; we had our own special Valentine's dinner. My relationship with my wife is basically just a friendship at this point. Today is a day where I don't know if I even want to give our marriage another chance. I guess that I should just focus on being friends again first, and then take it from there. I am still using the *2 Chairs* method of prayer time, talking and listening to God. I feel like He is telling me that my wife and I both need to focus on forgiveness. I believe that neither of us will receive the blessings we are asking for until we do. What are you harboring and holding on to? What is keeping you from finding God's blessing in your life?

Deep down inside I am starting to believe that this situation is something that I will be able to use to encourage other people. I don't know how many people cheat or get cheated on, but they all need to know that there is hope. I think that God wants to tell all of us a special message: if we start showing our faith in Him, then He will start showing His faith in us. If we put our hope in Him, then He will fill us with hope. If we take our weight and burdens to Him, He will bring us the freedom and peace that we are looking for. I feel like I've been waiting on Him to make my pain go away, but maybe He is waiting for me to actually hand it over to Him.

The ball is in our court, and we have to pass it to the person we trust the most or keep holding it for ourselves. I think that I will have to hand it over to God each time it comes up, but I think it will get easier and easier. The more I practice passing the ball, the better I'll get at it.

I still don't know when and where this story will end, but I still have hope. My wife wants some space so I'm going to give it to her, but sometimes I just want to hear her voice. I still love her. I definitely feel like a victim right now, that is just how I feel. If she wanted to get back together then I would do it. At the moment, the divorce is still on and we are slowly approaching the day when it becomes final. I wish we would have gotten divorced earlier instead of dragging this out and getting involved with another person. If things are bad, then we should fix it or end it, but don't string it along. I am trying to let go of the anger and pain, but I am also feeling defeated and depressed. It is hard not to feel that way as I soak in the consequences of everyone's actions. However, I know that God doesn't want us to go around feeling defeated and depressed; He wants us to enjoy life and truly experience His blessings. Sometimes it is a choice to be happy. Our happiness may just be a decision away. You can't always choose to make depression go away, but you can find some silver linings and focus on better things.

CHAPTER TWELVE

KISMET

March 3rd, 2019

I have been getting up really early these past couple of days. It is currently 3:37am and I am sitting in my soon to be ex-wife's house. She is sick and I have been staying over here for the past few nights to help take care of things. We are sleeping together; I'm just trying to be a good husband while I can be. The divorce is scheduled to finalize on April 1st, 2019. I am also trying to be a good father and help take care of my girls. It is definitely weird to be here and be in a situation like this, but I am thankful for it. I'm not sure why I'm getting up so early, but I am trying to make the most of my time. Love doesn't just go away, even in hard situations. So, I'm using my time to exercise my love.

It has been months without drinking and I'm feeling great. I have lost over 30 pounds since I have stopped drinking and my body looks and feels better than it has in decades. I've been buying protein bars, the chocolate brownie flavored ones, to eat every day. I was out yesterday to get some more when I saw this book stand right by the protein bars. This book caught my eye; it is called "Forgiving What You'll Never Forget". It felt like God placed this book right in front of me. It wasn't the only book on the display but it was the only one I saw, if that makes sense. It felt like divine intervention. I am excited to be reading through it. And I am excited to continually feel like God is putting things, people and opportunities in front of me to inspire and encourage me. I had another great moment a few days ago that is still making me smile.

I have been working on landscaping and trees for over 21 years now. I own and run this business and it is what pays most of my bills. Sometimes, to find more business, I will drive around and look for houses that might need some work done. I recently came across this nice house that had recently been sold. The seller had a ton of stuff out by the street, appearing to be giving or throwing it all away. So, I stopped my car and walked up to meet this guy. He told me his name was Lance and we ended up talking for a while. I mentioned to Lance that my company also offers a move-out cleaning service, which means we will remove remaining furniture off the property and clean the empty house. We ended up coming back a few days later to do the clean out service for his house. Good business but not a big deal, right? Now, watch what happens.

I continue talking with Lance and find out that he is a music producer. Pretty cool, especially because I have done some studio recording before and have a huge passion for music. So, Lance is a 71-year-old man with an eye patch. He looks like he is ready for retirement and he was in the process of downsizing his home. As it turns out, Lance was a producer for Bon Jovi, with multi-platinum records! The studio where I tried recording in the past shut down, and I had given up any interest in recording or releasing any music. But here I am, talking with a highly successful music producer who is now becoming a regular client of mine.

A little time went by but I kept in touch with Lance. One day I contacted him to see if he had any recommendations for a quality studio in the area where I could get back into recording. He gave me a name and that was that, until a few days ago when he called me. Normally I wouldn't have been available at that time, but it just so happened that I was free to take his call. Lance needed some help transferring items from one storage space to another. As we went through the items in storage we found issues of his platinum records. There were the Bon Jovi records as well as work from one of the Star Wars soundtracks. It was incredible to see all of his accomplishments that were just hanging out in a storage room. I can't believe he didn't mention working on Star Wars that is pretty awesome!

When my friend Ryan and I went to drop off the items at Lance's new home, we found one of the best home music studio set-ups that I have ever seen. Ryan and I have played music together for a long time and he has played guitar for my demo in the past. Suddenly Lance grabs a guitar and hands it to Ryan, he said, "Show me what you've got." We tried to give a few excuses as to why weren't ready to play and sing but Lance replied, "No excuses, just give me what you got." So, Ryan started to play and we started to sing. Lance listened and when we were finished he asked for another song, so we gave him one. His feedback was really positive and encouraging, he said that the song writing was great and the songs were the type that "people would love." I asked him about my singing and he gave me a few compliments, which meant a lot. I haven't always gotten the best feedback from certain people who were close to me, so this was some heartwarming validation for me.

Our Friday, which started with a small moving project ended with an audition with an accomplished music producer. He ended up giving us a challenge and some homework to do. He told us that we needed to practice at least three times a week for a month or so and then we could come back and record those songs. As we stayed and talked for a while, I told Lance that I believed that our meeting was not an accident; I felt like our paths crossed for a reason. He said, "Oh, like kismet!" I had to look up what that word meant, and I would normally use divine intervention but I like the word kismet better for this. God knew I needed some encouragement, something to enjoy and feel proud of. Not sure if this will lead to anything, but I will always have this moment as a reminder that anything is possible and God can guide us to blessings when we least expect it.

I genuinely don't feel happy that my wife is sick; I want her to feel better. However, I can also look at this as a little bit of kismet, that I could be home this morning to care for her and hold her when I would have otherwise been alone back at my place. Who knows what could pull us back together. I could keep on writing but right now I want to go snuggle up to her and be there when she wakes up this morning.

March 7th, 2019

I had a weird dream last night. I was in a gymnasium watching my older brother wrestle. I was going on to wrestle after him and I had this feeling that someone had come to support me and cheer for me like I was cheering for my brother. It was this woman, someone I don't know but she was there for me. She seemed strong. It is interesting that when I woke up, I was immediately comparing this unknown dream girl to my wife, who is also strong. I don't know if the girl in my dream is someone else, or maybe a dream version of my wife. I suppose that I desire to have a partner who is going to be here to watch me and support me and cheer me on. Maybe that is the point of my dream.

I have other dreams. Dreams of writing more books and even writing more screenplays. I dream that they could become successful, sell millions of copies, and help lots of people. Maybe I need to get an agent to help promote my work and help new projects get off the ground. Maybe I just need to keep doing what I'm doing and it will all take care of itself. In my *2 Chairs* time, I felt like God was affirming my heart for how I was staying strong in sobriety and handling things with my family. I wouldn't say that I've gotten straight A's, but maybe some solid B's. I actually started to cry because for a long time I was unsure of how I was doing. So having this peace from God that I was doing a good job meant a whole lot. It was more wind in my sails, a cool breeze on a hot summer afternoon.

I want to introduce and share a new element of my life with you. It is called kratom. Kratom is in the coffee family, it is a tropical evergreen tree from Asia. I've been taking it with a morning cup of tea each morning for a while. It has some benefits that have worked very well for me. However, you should know that it is currently a controversial substance. While it does have some benefits, there are also some side effects if you take too much. It is being looked into more and more, hopefully so that it becomes better regulated and more widely approved for purchase and consumption. It is perfectly legal in the state of Florida and I've been very thankful for the benefits. Again, taking the right amount and understanding your body's reaction to new things is very important. It has been part of my growing daily routine and overall I am feeling really great with where I am in my journey of recovery from alcoholism! My diet has grown as well. I eat a lot of protein but my body always craves sugar. For that I eat 3-4 protein bars a day. And almost like clockwork, ice cream almost every night.

March 9th, 2019

I went and opened up the yoga studio early this morning. I swept the floors and emptied all the trash. I had my *2 Chairs* prayer time and I'm just thankful for how I was feeling right now at this time and place in my life. I spent most of my prayer time telling God what I am thankful for. It has really put my heart and mind in a good place. I think it is so important to take time to recognize all of the good things in life that you are thankful for. The more aware we are, the more gratitude and joy we can feel. So try this, use a little space on this page or somewhere else and write down seven things that you are very thankful for. You might want to consider keeping that list somewhere you can see it, like on your dashboard or on the refrigerator. Be thankful and find ways to keep your thankfulness in front of you.

THE BIG TOE

There was another time that I experienced a kismet moment. I had previously played some semi-professional football. I was the kicker and played safety for our team. I would go out and kick an extra point barefoot, (that was just how I did it). An extra point is a pretty simple and routine part of football, but it does take a lot of coordinated efforts from the whole team to get that ball through the uprights. There is the snap, the hold, and the kick itself—but there are also a handful of guys who need to make and hold their blocks so that the defenders don't come in and block the kick.

Well, one night I went out for an extra point kick and one of my teammates apparently didn't think his block was important so the defender rushed right by him. The defender dove at the ball as I was kicking and my bare foot went straight into his shin. The next day I went to the hospital to find that my big toe was broken and would require nine months of rehab in order to properly heal. I started my landscaping business while finishing my rehab; I never went back to playing football. I would often think of that guy who didn't block for me and blame him for my pain and situation.

Later on, I was visiting a church that we normally don't attend. I was there to listen to the preacher; he was the father of one of the kids that I coached in wrestling. Before he got up to preach, another guy came up and talked for a couple of minutes. There was something about him that was familiar to me but I couldn't figure out what it was. After the service, I asked the preacher about him. He said, "I'm not sure how you would know him, although he did play semi-pro football." Then it hit me like a hurricane. He was my former teammate, the guy who didn't block for me on the extra point!

What is most incredible is that in that moment I immediately learned a few things. My toe didn't hurt anymore; I had even forgotten what the pain actually felt like. I also wasn't as mad at this guy as I had been before. Seeing him in a regular situation and not just as the idiot from the extra point also helped me. It also gave me an opportunity to acknowledge that I felt better and that I wasn't as mad at him as I thought I was.

Remembering that story definitely gives me hope for my marriage. The pain can go away, for both of us. There will come a time when we aren't as mad as we were. And it still seems like God has a way of bringing people and situations into our lives that will help us heal if we let them. If you have hurt someone, then you might always avoid them because you are afraid that they will never forgive you. Or if someone has hurt you, then you might avoid them because you don't want to confront anyone or deal with what has happened. But it can be a blessing to find yourself face-to-face with the person you said you never wanted to see again. It gives you a chance to forgive, be forgiven, see that the pain is in the past and move on. I'm glad I got this opportunity to do that, and I'm glad that my big toe is feeling better.

March 13th, 2019

Our cat has been missing for five weeks but was just seen a mile away. The girls and I traveled around the neighborhood calling for him to come home. I was worried about little Skippy Lou, but I knew that he was a resilient little animal and he was finding ways to stay alive. Soon after walking and yelling out his name on this quiet morning, I heard the sound of a cat meowing. It was coming from the sewer. I ran over and called out his name again. Suddenly, our little cat jumped out of the sewer and came right to us. My daughters cried tears of joy; it was a great way to start our day.

I'm still on the countdown leading up to April 1st, the day I'll be a single man. That is "April Fool's Day" and I can't help but see the irony in this. My wife has started saying that she still loves me, and I still love her, but we are not getting back together. The joke seems to be on both of us. It hurts thinking about saying good-bye once and for all. It is strange that we are getting along so well as we approach the divorce. Maybe she just wants to get there smoothly and then never talk to me again. Or maybe she is having second thoughts about splitting up. I guess only she knows at this point. All I know is that our cat found its way back to us after five weeks of being out on his own. He survived the elements, coyotes, snakes and the need for food and water. If he can be that resilient, then maybe I can too.

CHAPTER THIRTEEN
NOT THE END

March 22nd, 2019

We are now less than two weeks away from our divorce. We are drifting apart in some regards but still close in some ways. We aren't communicating very well but we are still physically near each other, except when she is out of town on business. We watched a movie with the girls and went to bed together tonight. I'm up late reflecting on the day and feeling hopeful that we just might make it through this. I know this book is nearing its end and I can't help but wonder what is coming next for us.

I've been sober for nearly half a year now! I am so thankful and proud to be able to say that. This is a major step and victory for my journey and me. I've been steering my life in the right direction and making daily decisions to help me on my way. My mission statement is feeling strong and all things are possible. God has brought me this far. You might have thought that my failing marriage would have dragged me back under, but here I am. I know that the disappointment and depression that I've felt at times could influence me, but I've tried to block that out from my heart. So, how is this supposed to end now? Where do we go from here?

March 25th, 2019

One week until April Fool's Day, the day our marriage ends. There are some financial situations involved in our pending divorce and I don't know how to feel about it. Basically, after liquidating some assets we will each have some money in our pocket. On one hand, it is real compensation for this to become an official split. On the other hand, it is a really small compensation for splitting up with your wife. There shouldn't be a dollar amount that justifies splitting up for good or makes it completely worth it. I've read about billionaires getting divorced and their spouses getting half; that is a massive amount of money that they are receiving but on some level it can't cover the dreams and vows that are now lost. Some things in life shouldn't have a price tag on them. My wife has my heart more today than she did the day we got married. I don't want to let her go.

Don't let go of yourself. You don't know what is around the corner. I had a friend try to commit suicide around the time that I Baker Acted myself. I wish he had done what I had done, but he made a different choice. He convinced himself to let go of everything, including his own life. He put a gun in his mouth and pulled the trigger. I couldn't imagine the place you have to be in to do that. But God has a different plan for his life and he survived his suicide attempt. I feel like I have a chance to help him realize that his life matters, that God is near and will help him pick up the pieces of his life. There will come a day when he will see things more clearly, even if it's uncertain right now. I think that we will all find some kind of better ending, or at least a better chapter.

March 30th, 2019

We are two days away from our divorce and we are getting along great. I am once again trying to focus on the blessings of life that are all around me. I also decided to go back and take my test again from earlier in this book. I am looking through my life to grade my faith, health, family and career. I gave myself a couple of 9 out of 10's and my score is really high for someone who is about to get divorced. Everything is going well right now. I am helping coach in the Special Olympics later today at a county meet. It is really early in the morning again, so I'm going to get back into bed and hold my wife while I still can.

Maybe you should test your score again and see if your score has changed at all since you started reading this book. You just might be surprised to see where you have improved and where you haven't. Make sure to always give yourself honest answers so you get clear opportunities to celebrate improvement and clear opportunities to make improvements.

MOSTLY DIVORCED
April 2nd, 2019

The day came and went; the divorce is final. I have to say, it was very anticlimactic. The process is very cold and unfeeling, like it isn't a big deal. But to me it is a big deal! As we were leaving the court, my ex-wife mentioned that she doesn't feel any different. So, I took off my wedding ring and threw it in the bushes. She started to cry and ran over to the bushes to retrieve my ring for me. I couldn't go along with the idea that this was no big deal and that nothing has changed. I just wanted to make a point that this is real and it is going to impact all of us. I gave her my last thoughts on our divorce and the events that brought us to this moment.

I got the money from the divorce quickly, but my ex-wife said that if I gave it back she would marry me that day. Again, this isn't that much money so it isn't about the dollars. She says she wants us to work again. I don't know how to feel about it. We talked about some ground rules about communication, fidelity and other things. It feels a little messed up right now. Am I supposed to put the ring back on? I still don't know where this is going but I hope you stay to come along for the ride with us!

PICKING UP THE PIECES

It is another day, and another early morning for me. Writing really helps me put my thoughts in order and sort out some of my feelings. I took my ex-wife out to eat and we brought the meal back to my place. I will say that my ex-wife and I had an intimate night back at my place. She seems really upset over the divorce, I think she knows that she could have stopped it but for whatever reason she didn't. We still have several arguments and fights over the divorce and past decisions that we both have made that hurt each other. Obviously, we have a lot to work out. My ex-wife started reading this book and it has brought up some good and bad emotions for her.

I just hit seven months sober! I've said it before but we both know that I've had lots of reasons to start drinking again but I haven't. I think that I have really changed, and I think more people are seeing that. More people are also praying for my ex-wife and I. I'd say we both feel like our hearts are slowly changing. I woke up this morning and felt so good about myself. I have drastically improved my health and fitness; it is hard not to feel proud about my body and the results I'm seeing from making healthy choices. I still enjoy things like ice cream almost every night, but my other choices have allowed me to enjoy something like that and still have great health. I've found a great balance in my diet and I'm just thankful for my good health; it really makes all the difference in how you feel.

It has been over a week since the divorce and I'm happy to say that my ex-wife and I are now dating. I'd say that we are boyfriend and girlfriend now. She gave me a list of things that she expects from me if we are ever going to get remarried. Right now I just want to take things slowly and continue working on my life. I've already improved so much by doing what I'm doing; I don't want to mess anything up by moving too fast. By the end of April we are doing yoga classes together, dating, and enjoying things like the Blueberry Festival in Brooksville, Florida.

I decided to try to grade myself again to see where I'm at on things. My score is the highest that it has ever been. Everything is going so well. I am so thankful to God for helping us pick up the pieces. No matter what you are going through, He can fix it; you just have to ask for His help.

SHE QUIT DRINKING
July 2nd, 2019

My girlfriend and I were talking about some of the decisions that were made in the past. I asked her if she thinks that she would have cheated on me if alcohol wasn't involved and she said, "No, no way!" So alcohol has caused us both problems and pain. There is a reason why they call it "spirits"; alcohol makes you say and do things that aren't who you really are. It takes you places you never intended to go and you cross lines that you never wanted to cross in a million years. But God can restore anything in our life. My girlfriend has changed a lot over the last month, all in good ways. She wants to change jobs, leaving a stable income for something that will be healthier for her and our family. Then, out of nowhere, she announced that she was going to quit drinking and she did. I am so proud of this woman!

I recently got back from California where I was visiting my older daughters at college. I was so happy to see them and I am so proud of them and the lives that they have created for themselves. While I was there, something pretty cool happened. California was where I lived when I went through my first divorce; it was a heartbreaking experience and I relocated to Florida to get away from it all.

My first wife left me and ended up with another guy. That all happened about sixteen years ago. Fast forward to this trip. I heard that my first ex-wife had divorced the guy she married; I had his number and I decided to reach out to him while I was in California. I asked him if he wanted to play golf with me and he said that he was in!

The only problem was that I didn't have any clubs. Well, we had also connected with my ex-wife's parents; I had always enjoyed their company and truly missed them. We talked for a while and I told my ex-father-in-law that I was playing golf the next day and he offered to let me play with his golf clubs. I was shocked!

So, I can sincerely say that I had a great trip connecting with my older daughters in California. Then I connected and caught up with my ex-wife's parents. Then I had a great time playing golf with the man who married my ex-wife, and I played with my ex-father-in-law's golf clubs. So, I know that God can heal anything. I was able to let go of some long held anger towards the man who my wife left me for. They were now divorced and I could only imagine that he was dealing with some of the same pains that I had dealt with. We didn't dive into a lot of personal details but I think just being together and having a good time was exactly what we both needed to heal. I was able to tell him about my journey with sobriety, getting healthy, and writing this book. It is funny to see how God works, especially because we don't understand it at first.

HAPPY BIRTHDAY TO ME
July 8th, 2019

Today is my 50th birthday. My girlfriend (ex-wife) and I got up early to enjoy each other's company before she had to run in to work. I am feeling really lucky today, and I can't wait to see what the next 50 years has in store for me.

Yesterday, we had an abundance of waves on the beach. We all had a blast on the boogie board, took some great pictures that I'm sure we will post on Facebook later. Not sure if I hate or love social media, but I do know that it feels good to get some "likes" on your post. I guess that all has to do with our desire to be wanted and liked by someone else. When you think about it, God is always there for us and is always cheering us on. He sees us and likes us, but He also sees everything and knows the messier parts of our lives. Could you imagine posting everything on social media, even the bad stuff?

Maybe we should consider that; consider living your life as if all of your actions and choices matter and not just the good ones that you show off online. God sees it all; your family and friends see more than you think. Who are you really trying to impress with the occasional posts of success? I think we all know that real change, real success, can only be shared and felt on a more personal level. That God, family and friends are the best people to know and celebrate you. I'm not at all saying social media is bad, I'm just thinking that sometimes we try too hard to show a perfect side of ourselves instead of actually committing to consistently being a better person.

I don't post my worst days or worst photos on Facebook, and you shouldn't either. We should just be careful not to pretend that our life, or the life of someone who has a "perfect" profile online, has no room to improve. And we shouldn't look at it as a platform to win people's admiration or approval, because God already loves us.

NOT THE END

In my drinking years, I had a lot of great things happen to me. Most of us will go through struggles and seasons of addiction and still find that there are blessings for us. I had all of my kids, who I love so much, during my long relationship with alcohol. I found love in the form of a beautiful woman who married me and is now my girlfriend. I started businesses and helped provide for my family. There were lots of great things that happened during those thirty years of drinking. However, I couldn't always fully enjoy or appreciate those blessings because of the addiction and dependency that I had with drinking.

I believe that the Devil tries to rob us of our joy and our blessings with vices like alcohol. His riptides are not always obvious; he might be pulling you out to sea and you don't even realize it yet. No one plans on becoming an alcoholic, cheater, liar, drug abuser or thief. I believe that we drift into those behaviors when we let our guard down and get caught in the current. If we take our eyes off the shore, or off the horizon, then we won't notice how far we have drifted until it is too late and we have been carried to a place and action that we never originally desired to make. That might be where you are now, but it doesn't have to be where you stay forever.

At any point, no matter how far out you've been pulled, you can make a change. You can employ Jesus Christ as your captain and let Him help you sail to better waters. You can evaluate and grow the four main areas of your life, slowly increasing your score as you regain health and confidence in yourself. You can find a mission statement that better defines you and directs your path. You can find forgiveness for yourself and for others who have hurt you. You can fall along the way, hit rock bottom, and get back up again. Everything in my life has changed. My story is far from perfect but I hope that makes you feel more hopeful. I still don't know where this life will take me, but I know who the captain of my ship is. In this life, I am currently living back with my ex-wife who is now my girlfriend. Not sure where this wave is going but I'm going to enjoy the ride that I'm on and continue to watch my life change and grow.

ANOTHER RIPTIDE

Last week on the 17th of September I celebrated an entire year of sobriety. Unfortunately, the following week I found out something I didn't want to know. All along, my ex-wife was saying that my drinking was the main reason for her unfaithfulness. Unfortunately, I regret to tell you that despite my sobriety, she did it again. This time she told me immediately after it happened. I was in total disbelief and believe it or not, so was she. Can you guess what she also started doing during the week leading up to it? Yep, she fell off the wagon and began drinking again. She slowly fell back into the same vicious cycle. This particular situation brings me back to the part in this book where I talk about the law of association. I used to associate drinking with sex. And it seems this is something her conscious or subconscious is also doing. So you know what I did? I put a ring back on her finger. Yep, we're engaged once again. If God can forgive David for what he did, then I can forgive the one I love also. Not sure how this is all going to play out but for now, by the Grace of God, just two weeks later I have forgiven her. Call it Godlike or stupidity. Didn't I mention this book was about forgiveness? She's my girl! I love her. In life I have learned there will always be Riptides and Tailwinds but I know God will get me through this because I can feel the Tailwinds coming. And if there is ever a person in this world that has a reason to drink, I'm pretty sure that guy would be me, but nope, not a drop! But I will have some ice cream! That is where I was going to end this story. But God had a different plan, a better plan!

BONUS CONTENT

I've written this section in screenplay format to set the scene for my soon-to-be Agent/Public Relationship manager.

Int: Grace Family Church

Date: 10-13-19 Sunday service

Main Character, Bradley Schenk and his fiancé Christina are seated in the back of the church. Their kids are in class while Bradley and Christina listen to the sermon. At the end of the sermon, the pastor presents an altar call. (An alter call is an invitation to receive Jesus Christ as Lord and Savior). Christina reaches over to Bradley, grabs his hand and starts to walk down to the altar. As they are walking down, Bradley notices the tears rolling down Christina's face. They stand in front of over 1,500 people next to Pastor Craig. Overwhelmed by the circumstance, Bradley begins to have tears in his eyes as well while still holding her hand. The pastor prays. Christina and Bradley repeat the prayer together.

PASTOR CRAIG, CHRISTINA AND BRADLEY

Jesus Christ I ask you to forgive me of all my sins; I want to start a new life. A life with you as my Lord and Savior! Come into my heart and life; I make you my Lord and Savior.

Bradley and Christina hug and kiss. The elders and Pastor hug them and congratulate them for making the most important decision any person can make in their life.

They walk out together to get their daughters, Adison and Ava, from class. It just happens to be the baptism day. On 10-13-19 at Grace Family Church Christina and Bradley renew their lives to Christ and the Schenk family was baptized together. Once again by chance or kismet, Bradley's oldest brother Ed (Butch) took pictures and filmed it with Bradley's phone. When they walked out of the baptism pool, Butch hands them some towels to dry off and congratulates them.

END THE MOVIE and the end of this book!

I didn't see that coming or could have made that up! Only God could do that and He did!

What does God want for you? It's simple. He wants you to be blessed and healthy and happy. But it starts by you giving Him your life and making Him your Captain. We will all have "Riptides and Tailwinds" in our lives. When you make God your Captain, he will calm the rough waters and make them smooth once again. He can do anything—just look what he did in my life! He is just waiting for you to call on Him! Love you all and God Bless! Now it's time for ice cream!

Made in the USA
Lexington, KY
09 December 2019